D1085238

INTRODUCING
ISSUES WITH
OPPOSING
VIEWPOINTS®

Hunting

Lisa Idzikowski, Book Editor

GREENHAVEN
PUBLISHING

Published in 2019 by Greenhaven Publishing, LLC
353 3rd Avenue, Suite 255, New York, NY 10010

Articles in Greenhaven Publishing anthologies are often edited for length to meet page requirements. In addition, original titles of these works are changed to clearly present the main thesis and to explicitly indicate the author's opinion. Every effort is made to ensure that Greenhaven Publishing accurately reflects the original intent of the authors. Every effort has been made to trace the owners of the copyrighted material.

Library of Congress Cataloging-in-Publication Data

Names: Idzikowski, Lisa, editor.
Title: Hunting / Lisa Idzikowski, book editor.
Description: First edition. | New York : Greenhaven Publishing, 2019. | Series: Introducing issues with opposing viewpoints | Audience: 7-12 | Includes bibliographical references and index.
Identifiers: LCCN 2018020674| ISBN 9781534504226 (library bound) | ISBN 9781534504813 (pbk.)
Subjects: LCSH: Hunting—Moral and ethical aspects. | Hunting—Philosophy. | Hunting.
Classification: LCC SK35.5 .H86 2019 | DDC 639/.1--dc23
LC record available at https://lccn.loc.gov/2018020674

Manufactured in the United States of America

Website: http://greenhavenpublishing.com

Contents

Foreword   5

Introduction   7

Chapter 1: Why Do People Hunt?

1. Hunting Does Not Make Us Human   11
   Vern Loomis
2. Hunting Is a Tradition That Should Be Continued   16
   Raised Hunting
3. Hunting Animals Is More Respectful Than Breeding   23
   Them for Consumption
   Soňa Supeková
4. Humans Were Once at the Mercy of Wild Animals   29
   All About Wildlife
5. Hunting Is Natural, but Is It Moral?   33
   Joshua Duclos

Chapter 2: Is Hunting Justified Today?

1. Hunting for Sport Is Cruel and Unnecessary   40
   People for the Ethical Treatment of Animals
2. Hunting Can Save Wildlife   46
   Terry Anderson
3. There Is No Rationale for Hunting in Developed Nations   52
   In Defense of Animals
4. Humans Are the Leading Cause of Animal Extinctions   58
   World Animal Foundation
5. Hunting Revenue Contributes to Conservation Efforts   64
   Joe Hosmer
6. There Is No Need to Harm Animals   68
   Ashley Capps

Chapter 3: What Is the Future of Hunting?

1. Without Conservation Efforts Species Extinction   73
   Is a Threat
   Barry Yeoman
2. Hunting Makes Sense for Controlling Invasive Species   80
   Liza Lester

3. Tribal Societies Must Be Allowed to Hunt 85
   Survival International
4. Eco-tourism Should Replace Trophy Hunting 89
   Teresa M. Telecky
5. The Bush Meat Market Shows Hunting's Economic 94
   Importance
   Emily Sohn
6. Hunting Is Its Own Endangered Species 99
   Noble Research Institute
7. Tourism and Conservation Can Work Together 103
   United Nations Environment Programme

Facts About Hunting 107
Organizations to Contact 109
For Further Reading 113
Index 117
Picture Credits 120

Foreword

Indulging in a wide spectrum of ideas, beliefs, and perspectives is a critical cornerstone of democracy. After all, it is often debates over differences of opinion, such as whether to legalize abortion, how to treat prisoners, or when to enact the death penalty, that shape our society and drive it forward. Such diversity of thought is frequently regarded as the hallmark of a healthy and civilized culture. As the Reverend Clifford Schutjer of the First Congregational Church in Mansfield, Ohio, declared in a 2001 sermon, "Surrounding oneself with only like-minded people, restricting what we listen to or read only to what we find agreeable is irresponsible. Refusing to entertain doubts once we make up our minds is a subtle but deadly form of arrogance." With this advice in mind, Introducing Issues with Opposing Viewpoints books aim to open readers' minds to the critically divergent views that comprise our world's most important debates.

Introducing Issues with Opposing Viewpoints simplifies for students the enormous and often overwhelming mass of material now available via print and electronic media. Collected in every volume is an array of opinions that captures the essence of a particular controversy or topic. Introducing Issues with Opposing Viewpoints books embody the spirit of nineteenth-century journalist Charles A. Dana's axiom: "Fight for your opinions, but do not believe that they contain the whole truth, or the only truth." Absorbing such contrasting opinions teaches students to analyze the strength of an argument and compare it to its opposition. From this process readers can inform and strengthen their own opinions, or be exposed to new information that will change their minds. Introducing Issues with Opposing Viewpoints is a mosaic of different voices. The authors are statesmen, pundits, academics, journalists, corporations, and ordinary people who have felt compelled to share their experiences and ideas in a public forum. Their words have been collected from newspapers, journals, books, speeches, interviews, and the internet, the fastest growing body of opinionated material in the world.

Introducing Issues with Opposing Viewpoints shares many of the well-known features of its critically acclaimed parent series, Opposing

Viewpoints. The articles allow readers to absorb and compare divergent perspectives. Active reading questions preface each viewpoint, requiring the student to approach the material thoughtfully and carefully. Photographs, charts, and graphs supplement each article. A thorough introduction provides readers with crucial background on an issue. An annotated bibliography points the reader toward articles, books, and websites that contain additional information on the topic. An appendix of organizations to contact contains a wide variety of charities, nonprofit organizations, political groups, and private enterprises that each hold a position on the issue at hand. Finally, a comprehensive index allows readers to locate content quickly and efficiently.

Introducing Issues with Opposing Viewpoints is also significantly different from Opposing Viewpoints. As the series title implies, its presentation will help introduce students to the concept of opposing viewpoints and learn to use this material to aid in critical writing and debate. The series' four-color, accessible format makes the books attractive and inviting to readers of all levels. In addition, each viewpoint has been carefully edited to maximize a reader's understanding of the content. Short but thorough viewpoints capture the essence of an argument. A substantial, thought-provoking essay question placed at the end of each viewpoint asks the student to further investigate the issues raised in the viewpoint, compare and contrast two authors' arguments, or consider how one might go about forming an opinion on the topic at hand. Each viewpoint contains sidebars that include at-a-glance information and handy statistics. A Facts About section located in the back of the book further supplies students with relevant facts and figures.

Following in the tradition of the Opposing Viewpoints series, Greenhaven Publishing continues to provide readers with invaluable exposure to the controversial issues that shape our world. As John Stuart Mill once wrote: "The only way in which a human being can make some approach to knowing the whole of a subject is by hearing what can be said about it by persons of every variety of opinion and studying all modes in which it can be looked at by every character of mind. No wise man ever acquired his wisdom in any mode but this." It is to this principle that Introducing Issues with Opposing Viewpoints books are dedicated.

Introduction

"There are some who can live without wild things, and some who cannot...Like winds and sunsets, wild things were taken for granted until progress began to do away with them. Now we face the question whether a still higher 'standard of living' is worth its cost in things natural, wild, and free. For us of the minority, the opportunity to see geese is more important than television, and the chance to find a pasque-flower is a right as inalienable as free speech..."
—*Aldo Leopold*, A Sand County Almanac, *1949*

Hunting, chasing and killing wild animals whether for sport or for survival, is widely practiced around the world. The US Fish and Wildlife Service indicates that 11.5 million Americans hunt, and similar reports show that 7 million Europeans partake in the activity. At the same time, according to the World Wildlife Fund (WWF), relatively new data from comprehensive studies on the impact of hunting show that worldwide populations of vertebrates are on a course of precipitous decline. This data predicts an average decline of 67 percent from population levels of 1970 to the end of the present decade. WWF argues that humanity's negative impact on species must be reduced. Many factors contribute to the decline of these species, but food production to meet an expanding human population is causing overhunting, overfishing, and poaching.

In Africa alone, the elephant population has plummeted by about 111,000 animals in the last decade because of poaching. And estimates of elephant numbers in 2016 say that around only 415,000 of these animals range across Africa. WWF is not the only animal conservation organization that cries out for immediate action. PETA, People for the Ethical Treatment of Animals, is a well-known anti-hunting organization that vigorously defends the rights of animals against what it calls "a violent form of recreation."

On a basic level, the controversial issue of hunting can be analyzed from two opposing viewpoints. Opponents argue that hunting is unnecessary, cruel, and barbaric. Proponents maintain that hunting is natural, acceptable, and sometimes essential for survival. Both opponents and proponents offer arguments that appear rational and wise. It is clear from these two viewpoints that hunting is a controversial concern.

Evidence cited by archaeologists and anthropologists indicates that early humans were hunter-gatherers. They obtained sustenance from hunting, fishing, gathering plant foodstuffs, and scavenging. Throughout the world, some of these early people hunted large predators: woolly mammoths, woolly rhinoceros, giant elk and other Pleistocene giants. Other groups of humans hunted, trapped, and fished for smaller animals such as rabbits, squirrels, turtles, local fish, and other small wild game. Meat obtained and eaten in turn helped humans develop bigger brains, and eventually they grouped into highly organized societies. Along the way, these prehistoric people harnessed fire, which made their hunted meat easier to digest and even more beneficial as a source of nutrition.

In some parts of the world, small groups of humans still exist as hunter-gatherers, but for the most part, the development of agriculture and domestication of animals moved human society away from being dependent solely on hunting as a source of protein. Farmers raised livestock for food, although people still hunted wild animals. As time went by, different areas around the world depended more on agriculture and less on hunting. Some places developed systems where only people of high rank in society such as kings and other nobles hunted, and everyday members of societies were forbidden to hunt, trap, or fish on these exclusive lands.

Many years later and into modern times, people still hunted. Some, such as Charles Darwin and John James Audubon, carried on scientific research and discovery. Traveling through Kentucky in 1813, Audubon reported that the "air was literally filled with pigeons; the light of noon-day was obscured as by an eclipse; the dung fell in spots, not unlike melting flakes of snow" That would be no one's experience today, because passenger pigeons have been wiped out due to rampant overhunting. The twenty-sixth President of the United States, Theodore Roosevelt, was an avid hunter. Roosevelt believed himself to be a conservationist and sportsman-hunter. He wrote that "in a civilized and cultivated country wild animals only continue to exist at all when preserved by sportsmen." Roosevelt maintained that "the excellent people who protest against all hunting, and consider sports-men as enemies of wild life, are ignorant of the fact that in reality the genuine sportsman is by all odds the most important factor in keeping the larger and more valuable wild creatures from total extermination."

During this time, at the turn of the twentieth century, some hunters killed ridiculous amounts of wild creatures—almost anything that was alive. Roosevelt and many others felt strongly about conserving wild animals and wild lands. They started clubs and organizations aimed at encouraging responsible hunting and conservation. During his time in office, Theodore Roosevelt passed laws to create the National Park System in the United States and save wild ecosystems and habitat for animals.

Whether prehistoric hunters depending on animals for sustenance, or modern-day hunters growing up in families that have pursued hunting as a tradition for generations, many who hunt show respect for the animals they hunt. Prehistoric cave art illustrates this reverence. Ancient caves in France and Spain display numerous paintings of animals done by artists who demonstrated the special connection to the animals their societies hunted. And today there are many communities and groups of hunters that celebrate and honor Saint Hubertus, the patron of hunters.

On the flip side, just as many if not more organizations and individuals abhor and protest hunting. They maintain that humans absolutely do not need to hunt for subsistence. They cite statistics showing the decreasing numbers of hunters and the increased number of "wildlife watchers." They point to the fact that hunting has caused extinction of animal species in the past and is bringing species to the brink of extinction today. And they vigorously campaign against trophy hunting and "canned hunts" where individual hunters are guaranteed of bagging game.

Many knowledgeable individuals and organized groups argue for or against hunting. Interestingly both sides maintain that their actions are done because of an inherent love of animals and a wish to protect or conserve animal species. The current debate that surrounds the practice of hunting is explored in *Introducing Issues with Opposing Viewpoints: Hunting* and sheds light on this divisive and ongoing contemporary issue.

Chapter 1

Why Do People Hunt?

Most people today do not need to hunt animals in order to eat.

Hunting Does Not Make Us Human

Vern Loomis

"Hunting as a means of survival has given way to farming, to agriculture, to an industrial scale of food production."

In the following excerpted viewpoint, Vern Loomis analyzes many factors that appear to predispose humans to hunting. Loomis argues that at one time successful hunting was essential for the survival of our species. He goes on to address the justification that many hunters offer for their participation in the sport: that modern humans are alive because early humans became good at hunting, enough to sustain and improve the human race to its current state. The author rejects this interpretation of our history as hunter-gatherers, that the ability of hunting or food gathering is somehow genetically within all of us. He argues that hunting became less about survival a long time ago and asks the reader to consider why we would need to hunt today. Vern Loomis is an alumnus of Michigan State University and writes for a variety of publications.

AS YOU READ, CONSIDER THE FOLLOWING QUESTIONS:
1. According to the author, what role does free choice have in hunting?
2. Does genetics play a role in hunting according to the viewpoint?
3. What were the payoffs of a successful hunt for early humans?

"Why We Kill and Hunt," by Vern Loomis, Center for Humans & Nature. Reprinted by permission.

Early humans learned to kill animals that posed threats to their survival.

All of us are killers—it comes with being alive. We may not all hunt, but if we allow ourselves to be part of this civilization, then we partake of the killing that runs through it. We can move off the grid as far as we like, we can rail against any part of it we dislike, but if we haven't opted out completely, we're still here, a part of it. We've willingly accepted a ride—a ride that ends the lives of many things in its path. We share the reality, the responsibility. If we're here, there's no valid claim to innocence. We can acknowledge our participation though, and still ask a question. Yes, we kill, but why also hunt? Why avidly hunt and kill when it seems unnecessary?

[...]

Hunting made possible our species survival, our evolution. With relatively fragile bodies, hunting and survival favored the development of large thinking brains—brains that eventually took us to the top of the food chain. Those same brains have taken us into this modern, increasingly industrialized world. Hunting as a means of survival has given way to farming, to agriculture, to an industrial scale of food production. There are still parts of the world beyond the reach of industrialization, where hunting is for subsistence, but in our familiar modern world, even in most of our rural areas, hunting is rarely for physical need. So why do we do it?

[...]

We live in a land of opportunity, free to make choices. We are one land, but with many cultures, many values. The decision to hunt is one of those choices, and comes with positive and negative implications. On one hand, it lends images of ruggedness, power, and utilitarianism—an image of someone close to nature and not afraid to make use of it. On the other hand, the same choice conflicts with other values adhered to (at least superficially) by much of the larger society. The idea of fairness, respect, and kindness towards other life forms, seems at odds with modern hunting. When hunting is for true need, for survival, there seems to be little conflict. It's the hunting without need, the hunting which has become recreational, that brings conflict. This conflict of value stimulates argument and justifications. There are many.

It's an easy contradiction for hunters to point out. We live in a meat-eating society, but shrink from the reality of procuring it. We condone the endless march of animals through our slaughter houses, but would decline to ever visit one. For most, such a visit would be hellish, shocking, and mind numbing (even a ghostly internet visit, free of the sounds, free of the smell, is appalling). How can the same society be critical of a hunter walking into the woods and dispatching an animal in its natural surroundings? Isn't that scenario more humane than the other nightmarish scene?

[...]

Some assert we have a predisposition to hunt, that we are genetically coded to pursue and kill. Our ancestors certainly were hunters. We were not simply carnivorous, though. We hunted more as omnivores. We were, and still are, opportunists—eating whatever food type is available. We eat meat, but seem just as content to raise it, as opposed to chasing it. In the United States, less than 7 percent of the adult population consider themselves to be hunters. In other industrialized nations, the numbers are often less. Is that enough to point towards predisposition, that we are genetically coded to hunt? Maybe yes, maybe no—conjecture always seems to play a role in linking behavior to genetics. Perhaps the genetic urge is simply to seek food, rather than assigning a specific route to its source. In any case, the more we use genetics to rationalize human behavior, the further we find ourselves from the idea of free will. The further from free will we wander, the more we resemble the instinctual animals we hunt. Is that the argument being made—we are but instinctual animals; therefore it's futile and pretentious to behave otherwise? That direction seems to run counter to another justification made for hunting—the idea of "dominion." The divine granting of "dominion" would seem to imply that humans are distinct from other animals and not enslaved by instinct—that there are other facets of our being to recognize and nurture.

Somewhat related to the thought of a hereditary factor towards hunting is the idea of a transcendental link to our ancestors and to the prey we are hunting. It alludes to a spiritual or mystical awakening as we hunt, bringing a communion with our forbearers. The spirit of the animal may even be invoked, offering its respect to us for the honorable way we've dispensed of its life. It's a colorful, gratifying idea, but thankfully, not so widely claimed or at least spoken of in the field. It's an embellishment more readily found in hunting publications, or plied by media personalities who like to glamorize their hunting activities.

The idea that our hunt even resembles that of our ancestor's, let alone communes with it, is over reaching, to the point of silliness. Ten thousand years ago humans were already atop the food chain. With cunning insight and cooperation, with little more than sticks and stones, the first humans became the most dangerous hunters— more so than the largest carnivores. However, dominance wasn't synonymous with invulnerability. They hunted to survive, and when successful, were able to celebrate having food and clothing for a bit longer, enough to reach the next hunt. If unsuccessful, existence was put at risk. Injuries, hunger, and death were always lurking, always waiting.

[…]

We know our ancestors were hunters. We exist today because they were good at it. They were the strong, the providers, and the protectors. In the emerging modern, but preindustrial world, hunting and fishing were still of primary importance in food gathering, a means of survival. Two hundred years ago, life outside the city's boundaries still predicated subsistence hunting. One hundred years ago, the need still existed for many, but less so. In today's industrial world, with the advent of large scale farming, with mass transportation, with all the comforts of modern life available in all but the furthest corners, hunting is an activity of little importance in sustaining our physical bodies.

[…]

EVALUATING THE AUTHOR'S ARGUMENTS:

In this viewpoint, Vern Loomis delves into the subject of hunting, looking at it particularly as a survival necessity for early humans which is still practiced by choice, by some modern people. Does the author feel that hunting is essential today? How does he make his case? Back up your reasoning with quotes from the viewpoint.

Hunting Is a Tradition That Should Be Continued

"Hunting as a family is by no means a new tradition. In fact, it used to be one of several traditional American family values."

Raised Hunting

In the following viewpoint, Raised Hunting proposes that hunting is a long-standing tradition that is rooted in the traditional American family value system. The authors maintain that the tradition of hunting is valuable and should be continued, especially in the modern age of digital technology, when families struggle to spend time together, and people are not as in touch with nature as they once were. The authors provide ideas on how to reignite what they consider an American tradition. Raised Hunting is a site about an average American family that has used hunting as a platform to teach ethics and values. It includes a nonprofit that certifies individuals in bow hunter education.

AS YOU READ, CONSIDER THE FOLLOWING QUESTIONS:

1. Why is the tradition of family hunting so important according to the authors?
2. How is technology portrayed in this viewpoint?
3. Which one of the "how to begin a tradition" ideas seems most achievable, and why?

"How Family Hunting Traditions Make You Stronger," Raised Hunting, May 13, 2016. Reprinted by permission.

Some people believe that hunting is an activity that encourages families to spend time together in nature. Many hunters enjoy the intergenerational aspect of the sport.

Tradition. That single word is loaded with so many meanings and interpretations. Most of them start with friends and family members gathered around the table or doing a fun event together. But in this case, we're specifically talking about the family hunting tradition that's so strong at Raised Hunting. When a father, mother, and children can all get together and do anything these days, it should be appreciated. But when they all willingly choose to spend their limited spare time with each other outdoors in some potentially miserable conditions, then we're talking about something really special. How do these traditions start? What keeps them together instead of falling by the wayside in the face of hundreds of modern distractions? Let's explore this a bit further.

Hunting as a family is by no means a new tradition. In fact, it used to be one of several traditional American family values. But the rise of modern civilization and agriculture offered many "conveniences" that ultimately made hunting less important for families. As a result, it dropped away in popularity or practice for many years and it is just now making gradual comeback. So whether you want to call this resurgence in the family hunting tradition an old one or a new interpretation of it, it doesn't change the fact that it's extremely essential.

Why Are Family Traditions Important?

You might wonder why family hunting is such a big deal to begin with. Well there are several reasons. First, spending time with a group of like-minded individuals helps build a community of trust and belonging, which is critical for young children to feel. But it's infinitely more important for them to feel supported and guided by their parents. Likewise, it gives parents another way to teach and spend time with their kids. They grow up very fast, so taking time to do those things while they're younger will cement them in place for the future.

Speaking of which, many families have strong deer camp traditions that have continued for generations after they started. Usually, they consist of getting extended family members together each hunting season to camp out in tents, trailers, ice houses, or shacks.

Old relations recall details of past hunts, catch up on life, and make plans for the next day's hunting activities around a fire. And sure, maybe a tall tale is occasionally told. Traditions like this start with simply inviting everyone out during the hunting season to enjoy some family time. It doesn't take much effort, but they will quickly become one of the longest-lasting and most treasured family memories you'll have.

Also, spending time together hunting means that all parties get a break from today's technology. Whether we're referring to our cell phones, work emails, video games, or social media, we all need to unplug once in a while to reduce mental stress and reconnect with nature. There's no better way to do that than watching the sun come up and hearing the forest come alive within a blind or tree stand with your family nearby. That being said, there are a lot of technological advances that have helped the hunting community tremendously, with scent-eliminating Scent Crusher products, trail cameras, and advanced Nikon optics to name a few. The difference is that these items are being used as part of the overall hunting approach and not to just mindlessly scroll through the latest updates from long-lost high school classmates. When you're in the woods with the family, especially teenage children, make it a point to lead by example. Focus on teaching a new tracking skill instead of checking for messages on your phone.

Additionally, the hunting tradition is so critical for us to carry on to the next generation because hunter recruitment and retention are serious issues in today's world. The simple fact is that hunters are some of the world's best conservationists, spending millions of dollars each year to support wildlife management and habitat conservation work. As the traditional hunting crowd ages, there's a noticeable lack of younger hunters to fill this void. With fewer hunters buying licenses and specific wildlife stamps/initiatives, there will be fewer dollars to spend on keeping our wildlife populations healthy and balanced. That means our great American tradition could slowly disappear. By getting children involved at a young age and taking your family hunting as often as possible, you can teach them about the critical function they could serve to help continue the tradition.

How to Start a Family Tradition

Hunting traditions could include most activities from the planning stage to actual field adventures. You probably already have a few of these types of family traditions at home, but here are some ways you could start one if not. First, know that just one really fun event can get everyone so engaged and excited that they can't wait to do it again. Just one fun day in the woods. Maybe they'd like to repeat it tomorrow, next week, in a few months, or next year. It all depends on what the activity is. Here are a few example traditions that you could try out at home with your own family.

Each spring, make it an annual tradition to go shed hunting as a family. It's a great way to spend a beautiful spring day and burn some energy after a winter off. Make an entire day of it by bringing along a picnic if the weather's nice enough. You could all take bets on who's going to find the biggest shed, the most antlers, or the weirdest find. Kids usually love these kinds of competitions. And you might find it pretty fun yourself.

One of the most basic family hunting traditions you could start is a family bow practice session with your Bear Archery bows. Pick a designated day of the week from spring through hunting season to all carve out thirty minutes to fling some arrows at targets. You can make it fun and keep your kids' attention by developing some archery games. Most kids love a little competition, especially if there's a friendly prize in it for the winner.

If you're a landowner or lease some property where you can plant food plots as a family, make a tradition to all head out to the farm to get some work done. Get your family involved in the process by letting them choose the seed mix for an experimental plot you rotate every year. If they're interested, let them help plan new plots with you. And definitely let them help with the work if they're still excited about it! After your food plots have started growing, you could all head out on a Friday night to glass the fields for bucks. If it's a longer drive, make sure to bring some snacks to keep everyone happy along the way. Maybe treat them to ice cream on a particularly hot summer day. A little bribery won't ruin them.

If you're planning on doing some family hunting trips next year and would like to make it an annual event, gather everyone around the table to plan out the details. Talk about the clothing you'll need, the route you'll take, the animals you'll be hunting, and any other relevant topics. By including the whole family in the discussion, it will help everyone to feel like they're part of the group. There are lots of family friendly hunting lodges out there that offer family hunting vacation packages. Take advantage of them while you can, because schedules will only get busier over time.

Other Family Hunting Tips

Here are a few other recommendations that would help in your pursuit to build a new tradition. Make sure to take lots of pictures and videos to document your family adventures. There's nothing quite like looking back at your family's memories. Think about how special it is to you if you can view pictures of your grandparents and great grandparents doing the same activity from many years prior. It allows you to reflect on what's changed over time and what's stayed the same. You might be surprised.

Similarly, you should keep a short journal of your family tradition activities. Just like the pictures, it allows you to recall in vivid detail the outcomes of any specific hunting trip or outdoor adventure. Small, but important, details can easily disappear from our memories within a short period of time. After only a year, you'd be surprised at what you forget. But recording the basic details (e.g., who, what, when, where, etc.) in a notebook or on a computer can allow you to look back on a hunting trip from ten years past and recall the memory without any problems.

Above all, you need to keep things fun while doing all of this. Don't turn scouting trips into forced marches, and don't be too critical. If your kids want to rest and do an impromptu snack break, join them! If you can let loose and all enjoy some laughter, you'll be much more likely to form a lasting event that you can continue throughout your life.

Why Do These Traditions Work?

We asked earlier in the article why certain traditions stick, while others simply fade away, doomed to be a one-time event. Let's expand on that a little more. It's easy to ignore the importance of family traditions sometimes. Work, school activities, and other events get in the way and we can lose track of time pretty easily. But when you elevate activities into a true family tradition, it takes on a new meaning. It becomes a special time that nobody wants to miss out on. It becomes a special and cherished memory.

The tradition of hunting is a perfect activity for families to do together since it can involve anyone. All you need is some open space and willing family members. By starting these activities while your kids are young, they can develop unique lifelong skills that they'll appreciate forever. And as we discussed earlier, life will get in the way unless we fight back and carve out some time for tradition. Don't wait any longer.

EVALUATING THE AUTHOR'S ARGUMENTS:

Viewpoint author Raised Hunting uses personal experience to outline several ways to begin a family tradition that may lead to hunting. How does this personal approach make you feel about what the authors convey? Does it lead you to consider your own family traditions? Does it alter the way you might have thought before reading the viewpoint?

Hunting Animals Is More Respectful Than Breeding Them for Consumption

Soňa Supeková

"The community of hunters in most European countries consider hunting not only a hobby, but also a lifestyle and mission."

In the following viewpoint, Soňa Supeková depicts the tradition of hunting as it is still practiced in Europe. Supeková maintains that to be a respectful hunter, certain practices, cultural traditions, manners and behaviors must be followed. The author details her analysis with examples from own family and country of Slovakia. Supeková is vice dean of economics and business at the University of Bratislava, Slovak Republic. She is the founder and president of the Club of Slovak Lady Hunters and focuses her writing on the topic of European hunting traditions.

"Hunting Traditions in Europe—The Way of Life for Hunters," by Soňa Supeková, Center for Humans & Nature. This essay was originally published by the Center for Humans and Nature as part of their questions for a Resilient Future Series: Does hunting make us human? Reprinted by permission.

AS YOU READ, CONSIDER THE FOLLOWING QUESTIONS:
1. How does the author feel about hunting traditions?
2. According to the author, what happened in Slovakia after the two world wars?
3. According to the viewpoint, what segment of Europe's population is increasing in hunting?

I am hunter. I grew up in a hunting family. Most of my childhood was spent in the forest with my grandfather and father, the most important people in my life as a hunter. They taught me how to behave in nature and respect wildlife, and how important old hunting traditions are for us all.

Hunting is an inseparable part of life and has been since the dawn of humankind; it has, for example, assisted human development and progress. Hunting and all activities associated with it are very important intercultural phenomena—not only in Europe but throughout the world.

How did hunting and associated traditions develop in Europe? The community of and mission. For most of them, it is not just about the joy of the quarry, the kill, or the trophies; it is about the honor of being hunters. It is an honor to belong to a group of people associated with nature and its resources. Is there a simple answer to the question "Does hunting make us human"? No, but the answer can be found in European hunting traditions and in the way of life that hunters lead.

Hunters in Europe and around the world struggle daily with the media and especially with many non-hunters, particularly about whether their hobby and style of obtaining food is ethically and socially acceptable. So, what is more human: a) hunting deer in the woods in such a way that it does not feel threatened before the shot is fired, or b) breeding animals solely for meat and in often appalling conditions? This is a question that we hunters are asked on a daily basis by those who claim to be guardians of nature and of animals. Many of them have no idea what the role of hunters is in the forest and what tasks they need to carry out in hunting areas throughout

Traiditionally, European hunters show respect for their harvest by placing a sprig of evergreen in the animal's mouth to represent the final meal before consumption and to honor the land.

the year in order to be hunters. It is mostly hunters who call for the protection of endangered species, and equally it is often they who deserve credit for wildlife conservation.

An example of this is in my home country, Slovakia, where, after two world wars the state of wildlife was alarming. At that time, there were no conservationists, and the credit for the increasing game populations went to the hunters, who were already a well-organized group. Thanks to their excellent monitoring and sustainable wildlife management, it was possible for hunters to stop the decrease in game populations and, in fact, to increase their numbers.

Urbanization puts a great deal of pressure on the whole area of Central Europe. Wildlife here is under constant stress from increasing human populations and expanding industries and infrastructures. Throughout the area, there are only a few small patches of untouched nature. Today, therefore, the sustainable management of hunting is so important, and the respect for hunting traditions provides a bond between hunters and the landscape. This bond is preserved through the rituals and traditions associated with hunting.

The preservation of old hunting traditions starts with what is known as the "communion." This communion is the first of all hunters' moral and ethical promises to behave, with utmost respect, towards wildlife and nature. The basis of European hunting traditions and rituals is the respect towards wildlife and to the game that is caught. This "respect" is an important part of the hunter's life throughout the year, not just during the hunting season. Hunters manifest this respect in many places and manners: in nature, in the forest, through hunting, on social occasions, and also in their personal life. The sustainable use of wildlife and sustainable hunting management take place in the majority of European countries. Deer in the wild feel the stress of civilization. Hunters in Europe are amongst those best able to alleviate the pressures that are placed on wildlife. The reward for hunters is the opportunity to spend time in nature and to hunt. In turn, hunters also show the proper respect for wild game.

The clothing worn by European hunters when out hunting is also important. Even clothes used for working in nature are always green. For driven hunts, hunters are often dressed in uniform, and it is considered impolite to come wearing dirty boots or to be late. Driven hunts provide an opportunity for friendly gatherings, with all activities being announced by horn blowers and other hunting signals. After a hunt, whether an individual or driven hunt, hunters pay their respects to the game taken. During the closing ceremony— the game bag—the game is laid down, with its right side facing the ground, in a rectangle defined by pine branches. There are fires at each of the four corners. With this presentation, hunters say goodbye to the game and show their appreciation for nature. Each downed animal has a small branch most often from a pine tree, in its mouth representing its last bite. When taking the game from the place where it was caught, the hunters point the animal's head toward the natural area so that for the last time it can look at the place where it lived.

Women play a very important role in European hunting nowadays. In the past, women participated mainly in the activities that followed the hunt. In the countries of former Austro–Hungary, women participated in the social activities of hunting. In the 19th and early 20th centuries, hunting in Europe underwent a final development, and so-called "exclusive hunting" was transformed into a professional activity focused on breeding and the quality and comprehensive care for game animals.

Today, as more and more women work in positions and choose hobbies that were previously dominated by men, the number of active female hunters is constantly growing. In Austria, for example, there are more than 11,000 registered female hunters. Hunting is traditionally widespread in rural areas, and women in Austria increasingly hunt and participate in public hunting life. The number of registered huntresses in Eastern European countries is also increasing annually, although their activities are connected to events organized mainly by men. The Nordic countries, too, are well known for their high numbers of hunters per capita. For example, there are more than 15,000 registered woman hunters in Sweden.

Women also occupy an important place in falconry and hunting cynology, faring well in competitions and serving as judges of various dog events and field shows.

In addition, women are active in many areas related to hunting: education, work with children and with youth, shooting, and fashion. In the countries of Central and Eastern Europe, women regularly organize workshops—to which both men and women are invited—focused on processing and cooking wild game. They exchange recipes and host culinary competitions. Women help convey the elegance of hunting and inspire men to take greater care of their garments and uniforms. Some young women become hunters even without any such family tradition, often thanks to their partners.

When speaking about hunting traditions, one of the most important sustainable hunting organizations, which has its headquarters in Europe, is the International Council for Game and Wildlife Conservation (CIC). The CIC is a politically independent advisory body that aims to preserve wildlife through sustainable hunting. The CIC advocates for the sustainable use of wildlife resources and promotes, on global scale, sustainable hunting as a tool for conservation, while building on valued traditions.

EVALUATING THE AUTHOR'S ARGUMENTS:

Viewpoint author Soňa Supeková describes in reverent detail a view of the traditions of European hunting. Compare and contrast traditional European hunting with that presented in the previous viewpoint.

Humans Were Once at the Mercy of Wild Animals

"Much of the world's earliest art depicts drawing and painting of animals that we humans hoped would sustain us and keep us from hunger and cold."

All About Wildlife

In the following viewpoint, All About Wildlife introduces readers to prehistoric cave art. The author lightly details some of the most famous sites of cave art in the world, the artists, and the animals depicted in the art. According to the author, this art illustrates the respect that prehistoric hunters had for the animals that they killed in order to survive. They killed for the meat that would sustain them, and they killed in order to avoid being killed. It is important to remember that this was a time in which wild animals were a threat to human existence. These circumstances bred a deep respect in humans for wildlife. All About Wildlife is an online site published by Paul Guernsey, an environmental educator dedicated to providing a resource about animals.

AS YOU READ, CONSIDER THE FOLLOWING QUESTIONS:
1. According to the author, where is cave art found?
2. Who were the best cave artists, as stated in this viewpoint?
3. What are the three most famous caves for prehistoric art?

"The Earliest Wildlife Art," All About Wildlife, September 16, 2010. Reprinted by permission.

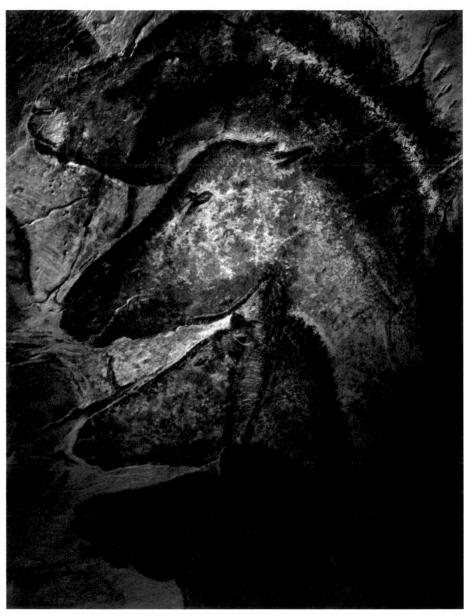

Prehistoric cave art, such as these paintings of horses on the walls of the Chauvet cave in France, tells us a lot about the importance of animals to our early ancestors.

It was not that long ago that wildlife meant everything to mankind. All humans sustained themselves through hunting animals, catching fish and gathering edible plants that grew naturally. For a lot of groups, when herds of wild game moved, it was necessary to move with them to avoid starvation. In fact, according to one widely-accepted theory, humans were drawn out of Africa to populate the rest of the world by migrating herds of big game.

It stands to reason, then, that something so central to our survival as wild animals would come to preoccupy much of our developing capacity for thought as well as to dominate our blossoming spiritual lives. In fact, even though much of humankind switched over to agriculture and a sedentary lifestyle many thousands of years ago, the visible proof for this supposition remains behind in caves and on the rock walls of sheltered cliffs the world over.

Much of the world's earliest art depicts drawing and painting of animals—many now long extinct—that we humans hoped—perhaps even prayed—would sustain us and keep us from hunger and cold. This wildlife art can be found almost everywhere that early humans traveled, from the cliff faces of the American West to the rocky outcroppings of Australia.

Some of the most accomplished artists were the stone-age Europeans known as Cro-Magnons, who were the direct ancestors of today's European peoples. Painting on the dark walls of caves, these artists created a highly detailed and extremely accurate pictorial record of the wildlife with which they found themselves surrounded. The damp conditions inside the caves did such a good job of preservation that many of these cave paintings look just as fresh today as they did the day—15- to 30,000 years ago—when they were first brought to vibrant life. Wild animals depicted in the lifelike paintings include horses, bears, European bison—now almost extinct—aurochs (the much larger ancestor of the modern bovine; now extinct); deer and even the extinct woolly rhinoceros.

Three of the most famous caves are Lascaux and Chauvet in southern France, and Altamira, in Spain. The picture on the previous page is one of the most famous of all the many Altamira paintings. Lascaux was discovered by a pair of French teenagers in 1940; its

2,000 paintings are estimated to be over 17,000 years old. Chauvet, not discovered until 1994 contains the most ancient Paleolithic art, estimated at over 30,000 years old. The paintings at Altamira in Spain, mostly of bison, are thought to be 20,000 years old. The cave was discovered in the late 1800's.

The early European artists created their cave paintings using charcoal and a variety of pigments found in the natural environment such as ochres (red and yellow), hematite and manganese oxide.

Cave art serves to remind us that there once was a time when we were at the mercy of wildlife, and not the other way around. The thought makes a wildlife appreciator feel wistful.

EVALUATING THE AUTHOR'S ARGUMENTS:

In this viewpoint, All About Wildlife author Paul Guernsey portrays the prehistoric hunter as an individual or group member that is honoring the animals they hunt. How does this compare to the hunting rituals of Slovakian hunters described in the previous viewpoint?

Hunting Is Natural, but Is It Moral?

"Hunters see the act of stalking and killing deer, ducks, moose and other quarry as humane, necessary and natural, and thus as ethical."

Joshua Duclos

In the following viewpoint, Joshua Duclos attempts to examine the topic of hunting from both sides—and also from the perspective of morality. In simple terms, hunters think the activity is necessary and natural, and nonhunters see it as cruel and useless. Duclos identifies three reasons to hunt and uses a philosophical approach to address the objections that nonhunters raise against the practice. Joshua Duclos is a PhD candidate in philosophy at Boston University and a backcountry guide in the White Mountains of New Hampshire.

AS YOU READ, CONSIDER THE FOLLOWING QUESTIONS:
1. What three rationales for hunting does the author present?
2. According to the author, what bothers people about hunting?
3. What is meant by saying that hunting is a natural activity as defined by this viewpoint?

Can big-game trophy hunting be justified? Critics argue that it is cruel and unnecessary. Proponents claim it can boost a region's economy.

Every year as daylight dwindles and trees go bare, debates arise over the morality of hunting. Hunters see the act of stalking and killing deer, ducks, moose and other quarry as humane, necessary and natural, and thus as ethical. Critics respond that hunting is a cruel and useless act that one should be ashamed to carry out.

As a nonhunter, I cannot say anything about what it feels like to shoot or trap an animal. But as a student of philosophy and ethics, I think philosophy can help us clarify, systematize and evaluate the arguments on both sides. And a better sense of the arguments can help us talk to people with whom we disagree.

Three Rationales for Hunting

One central question is why people choose to hunt. Environmental philosopher Gary Varner identifies three types of hunting: therapeutic, subsistence and sport. Each type is distinguished by the purpose it is meant to serve.

Therapeutic hunting involves intentionally killing wild animals in order to conserve another species or an entire ecosystem. In one example, Project Isabella, conservation groups hired marksmen to eradicate thousands of feral goats from several Galapagos islands between 1997 and 2006. The goats were overgrazing the islands, threatening the survival of endangered Galapagos tortoises and other species.

Subsistence hunting is intentionally killing wild animals to supply nourishment and material resources for humans. Agreements that allow Native American tribes to hunt whales are justified, in part, by the subsistence value the animals have for the people who hunt them.

In contrast, sport hunting refers to intentionally killing wild animals for enjoyment or fulfillment. Hunters who go after deer because they find the experience exhilarating, or because they want antlers to mount on the wall, are sport hunters.

These categories are not mutually exclusive. A hunter who stalks deer because he or she enjoys the experience and wants decorative antlers may also intend to consume the meat, make pants from the hide and help control local deer populations. The distinctions matter because objections to hunting can change depending on the type of hunting.

What Bothers People About Hunting: Harm, Necessity, and Character

Critics often argue that hunting is immoral because it requires intentionally inflicting harm on innocent creatures. Even people who are not comfortable extending legal rights to beasts should acknowledge that many animals are sentient—that is, they have the capacity to suffer. If it is wrong to inflict unwanted pain and death on a sentient being, then it is wrong to hunt. I call this position "the objection from harm."

If sound, the objection from harm would require advocates to oppose all three types of hunting, unless it can be shown that greater harm will befall the animal in question if it is not hunted—for example, if it will be doomed to slow winter starvation. Whether a hunter's goal is a healthy ecosystem, a nutritious dinner or a personally fulfilling experience, the hunted animal experiences the same harm.

But if inflicting unwanted harm is necessarily wrong, then the source of the harm is irrelevant. Logically, anyone who commits to this position should also oppose predation among animals. When a lion kills a gazelle, it causes as much unwanted harm to the gazelle as any hunter would—far more, in fact.

Few people are willing to go this far. Instead, many critics propose what I call the "objection from unnecessary harm:" it is bad when a hunter shoots a lion, but not when a lion mauls a gazelle, because the lion needs to kill to survive.

Today it is hard to argue that human hunting is strictly necessary in the same way that hunting is necessary for animals. The objection from necessary harm holds that hunting is morally permissible only if it is necessary for the hunter's survival. "Necessary" could refer to nutritional or ecological need, which would provide moral cover for subsistence and therapeutic hunting. But sport hunting, almost by definition, cannot be defended this way.

Sport hunting also is vulnerable to another critique that I call "the objection from character." This argument holds that an act is contemptible not only because of the harm it produces, but because of what it reveals about the actor. Many observers find the derivation of pleasure from hunting to be morally repugnant.

In 2015, American dentist Walter Palmer found this out after his African trophy hunt resulted in the death of Cecil the lion. Killing Cecil did no significant ecological damage, and even without human intervention, only one in eight male lions survives to adulthood. It would seem that disgust with Palmer was at least as much a reaction to the person he was perceived to be—someone who pays money to kill majestic creatures—as to the harm he had done.

The hunters I know don't put much stock in "the objection from character." First, they point out that one can kill without having hunted and hunt without having killed. Indeed, some unlucky hunters go season after season without taking an animal. Second, they tell me that when a kill does occur, they feel a somber union with and respect for the natural world, not pleasure. Nonetheless, on some level the sport hunter enjoys the experience, and this is the heart of the objection.

Is Hunting Natural?

In discussions about the morality of hunting, someone inevitably asserts that hunting is a natural activity since all preindustrial human societies engage in it to some degree, and therefore hunting can't be immoral. But the concept of naturalness is unhelpful and ultimately irrelevant.

A very old moral idea, dating back to the Stoics of ancient Greece, urges us to strive to live in accordance with nature and do that which is natural. Belief in a connection between goodness and naturalness persists today in our use of the word "natural" to market products and lifestyles—often in highly misleading ways. Things that are natural are supposed to be good for us, but also morally good.

Setting aside the challenge of defining "nature" and "natural," it is dangerous to assume that a thing is virtuous or morally permissible just because it is natural. HIV, earthquakes, Alzheimer's disease and post-partum depression are all natural. And as *The Onion* has satirically noted, behaviors including rape, infanticide and the policy of might-makes-right are all present in the natural world.

Hard Conversations

There are many other moral questions associated with hunting. Does it matter whether hunters use bullets, arrows or snares? Is preserving a cultural tradition enough to justify hunting? And is it possible to oppose hunting while still eating farm-raised meat?

As a starting point, though, if you find yourself having one of these debates, first identify what kind of hunting you're discussing.

If your interlocutor objects to hunting, try to discover the basis for their objection. And I believe you should keep nature out of it.

Finally, try to argue with someone who takes a fundamentally different view. Confirmation bias—the unintentional act of confirming the beliefs we already have—is hard to overcome. The only antidote I know of is rational discourse with people whose confirmation bias runs contrary to my own.

EVALUATING THE AUTHOR'S ARGUMENTS:

In this viewpoint, author Joshua Duclos approaches hunting from a philosophical perspective. Using examples from the viewpoint, construct an argument to persuade a hunter that hunting is not natural or moral.

Chapter 2

Is Hunting Justified Today?

Some cultures, such as the Inupiat Eskimo, still rely on subsistence hunting.

Hunting for Sport Is Cruel and Unnecessary

"Although it was a crucial part of humans' survival 100,000 years ago, hunting is now nothing more than a violent form of recreation"

People for the Ethical Treatment of Animals

In the following viewpoint, People for the Ethical Treatment of Animals (PETA) argues that, even though hunting was once an important form of survival, in modern times it is simply a violent form of recreation. PETA maintains that few people in the United States hunt for survival, although many animals are killed, maimed, and suffer needlessly because of sport hunting. PETA exposes a particularly cruel form of hunting—canned hunting—and demonstrates that it is big business. PETA, the People for the Ethical Treatment of Animals is a worldwide organization working on behalf of animal rights.

AS YOU READ, CONSIDER THE FOLLOWING QUESTIONS:
  1. Explain how PETA defines the "delicate balance of ecosystems."
  2. According to this viewpoint, what is a "canned hunt?"
  3. As stated by PETA, what can individuals do to support a no-hunting stance?

"Why Sport Hunting Is Cruel and Unnecessary," People for the Ethical Treatment of Animals, Inc. ("PETA"). Reprinted by permission.

Animal rights activists protested when an American dentist paid a large sum to a local guide to help him track and kill a lion in Zimbabwe.

Although it was a crucial part of humans' survival 100,000 years ago, hunting is now nothing more than a violent form of recreation that the vast majority of hunters do not need for subsistence.[1] Hunting has contributed to the extinction of animal species all over the world, including the Tasmanian tiger and the great auk.[2,3]

Less than 5 percent of the US population (13.7 million people) hunts, yet hunting is permitted in many wildlife refuges, national forests, and state parks and on other public lands.[4] Almost 40 percent of hunters slaughter and maim millions of animals on public land every year, and by some estimates, poachers kill just as many animals illegally.[5,6]

Pain and Suffering

Many animals endure prolonged, painful deaths when they are injured but not killed by hunters. A study of 80 radio-collared white-tailed deer found that of the 22 deer who had been shot with "traditional archery equipment," 11 were wounded but not recovered by

hunters.[7] Twenty percent of foxes who have been wounded by hunters are shot again. Just 10 percent manage to escape, but "starvation is a likely fate" for them, according to one veterinarian.[8] A South Dakota Department of Game, Fish and Parks biologist estimates that more than 3 million wounded ducks go "unretrieved" every year.[9] A British study of deer hunting found that 11 percent of deer who'd been killed by hunters died only after being shot two or more times and that some wounded deer suffered for more than 15 minutes before dying.[10]

Hunting disrupts migration and hibernation patterns and destroys families. For animals such as wolves, who mate for life and live in close-knit family units, hunting can devastate entire communities. The stress that hunted animals suffer—caused by fear and the inescapable loud noises and other commotion that hunters create—also severely compromises their normal eating habits, making it hard for them to store the fat and energy that they need in order to survive the winter.

Nature Takes Care of Its Own

The delicate balance of ecosystems ensures their survival—if they are left unaltered. Natural predators help maintain this balance by killing only the sickest and weakest individuals. Hunters, however, kill any animal whose head they would like to hang over the fireplace—including large, healthy animals who are needed to keep the population strong. Elephant poaching is believed to have increased the number of tuskless animals in Africa, and in Canada, hunting has caused bighorn sheep's horn size to fall by 25 percent in the last 40 years. *Nature* magazine reports that "the effect on the populations' genetics is probably deeper."[11]

Even when unusual natural occurrences cause overpopulation, natural processes work to stabilize the group. Starvation and disease can be tragic, but they are nature's ways of ensuring that healthy, strong animals survive and maintain the strength of the rest of their herd or group. Shooting an animal because he or she might starve or get sick is arbitrary and destructive.

Another problem with hunting involves the introduction of exotic "game" animals who, if they're able to escape and thrive, pose a threat to native wildlife and established ecosystems.

Canned Cruelty

Most hunting occurs on private land, where laws that protect wildlife are often inapplicable or difficult to enforce. On private lands that are set up as for-profit hunting reserves or game ranches, hunters can pay to kill native and exotic species in "canned hunts." These animals may be native to the area, raised elsewhere and brought in, or purchased from individuals who are trafficking in unwanted or surplus animals from zoos and circuses. The animals are hunted and killed for the sole purpose of providing hunters with a "trophy."

Canned hunts are big business—there are an estimated 1,000 game preserves in the US, with some 5,000 so-called "exotic ranchers" in North America.[12,13] Ted Turner, the country's largest private landowner, allows hunters to pay thousands of dollars to kill bison, deer, African antelopes, and turkeys on his 2 million acres.[14]

Animals on canned-hunting ranches are often accustomed to humans and are usually unable to escape from the enclosures that they are confined to, which range in size from just a few yards to thousands of acres. Most of these ranches operate on a "no-kill, no-pay" policy, so it is in owners' best interests to ensure that clients get what they came for. Owners do this by offering guides who are familiar with animals' locations and habits, permitting the use of dogs, and supplying "feeding stations" that lure unsuspecting animals to food while hunters lie in wait.

While many states have limited or banned canned hunts, there are no federal laws regulating the practice at this time.[15]

Other Victims

Hunting accidents destroy property and injure or kill horses, cows, dogs, cats, hikers, and other hunters. In 2006, then–Vice President Dick Cheney famously shot a friend while hunting quail on a canned hunting preserve.[16] According to the National Shooting Sports Foundation, thousands of injuries arc attributed to hunting in the US every year—and that number only includes incidents involving humans.[17]

The bears, cougars, deer, foxes, and other animals who are chased, trapped, and even killed by dogs during (sometimes illegal) hunts aren't the only ones to suffer from this variant of the "sport." Dogs used for hunting are often kept chained or penned and are denied routine veterinary care such as vaccines and heartworm medication. Some are lost during hunts and never found, whereas others are turned loose at the end of hunting season to fend for themselves and die of starvation or get struck by vehicles.

What You Can Do

Before you support a "wildlife" or "conservation" group, ask about its position on hunting. Groups such as the National Wildlife Federation, the National Audubon Society, the Sierra Club, the Izaak Walton League, the Wilderness Society, and the World Wildlife Fund are pro–sport-hunting, or at the very least, they do not oppose it.

To combat hunting in your area, post "no hunting" signs on your land, join or form an anti-hunting organization, protest organized hunts, and spread deer repellent or human hair (from barber shops) near hunting areas. Call 1-800-628-7275 to report poachers in national parks to the National Parks and Conservation Association. Educate others about hunting. Encourage your legislators to enact or enforce wildlife-protection laws, and insist that nonhunters be equally represented on the staffs of wildlife agencies.

Notes

1. National Research Council, "Science and the Endangered Species Act" (Washington, D.C.: National Academy Press, 1995), p. 21.
2. Grant Holloway, "Cloning to Revive Extinct Species," CNN.com, 28 May 2002.
3. Canadian Museum of Nature, "Great Auk," 2008.
4. US Fish and Wildlife Service, "2011 National Survey of Fishing, Hunting, and Wildlife-Associated Recreation" (Washington, D.C.: GPO, 2012), p. 22.
5. US Fish and Wildlife Service, 28.
6. Illinois Department of Natural Resources, "How the Program Works," accessed 25 July 2013.
7. Stephen S. Ditchkoff et al., "Wounding Rates of White-Tailed Deer With Traditional

Archery Equipment," Proceedings of the Annual Conference of the Southeastern Association of Fish and Wildlife Agencies (1998).

8. D.J. Renny, "Merits and Demerits of Different Methods of Culling British Wild Mammals: A Veterinary Surgeon's Perspective," Proceedings of a Symposium on the Welfare of British Wild Mammals (London: 2002).

9. Spencer Vaa, "Reducing Wounding Losses," South Dakota Department of Game, Fish, and Parks, accessed 25 July 2013.

10. E.L. Bradshaw and P. Bateson, "Welfare Implications of Culling Red Deer (Cervus Elaphus)," Animal Welfare 9 (2000): 3–24.

11. John Whitfield, "Sheep Horns Downsized by Hunters' Taste for Trophies," Nature 426 (2003): 595.

12. Morgan Loew, "Arizona Organization Protects 'Canned' Hunting," CBS5 9 Nov. 2012.

13. CBS News, "Can Hunting Endangered Animals Save the Species?" *60 Minutes* 29 Jan. 2012.

14. Robert M. Poole, "Hunters: For Love of the Land," *National Geographic Magazine* Nov. 2007.

15. Morgan Loew, "Arizona Organization Protects 'Canned' Hunting," CBS5 9 Nov. 2012.

16. Dana Bash, "Cheney Accidentally Shoots Fellow Hunter," CNN.com, 12 Feb. 2006.

17. National Shooting Sports Foundation, "Firearms-Related Injury Statistics," Industry Intelligence Reports, 2012.

EVALUATING THE AUTHOR'S ARGUMENTS:

In this viewpoint, PETA claims that many conservation organizations such as the National Audubon Society do not oppose sport-hunting. Why might conservation groups take this stance?

Viewpoint

2

Hunting Can Save Wildlife

Terry Anderson

"While it is true that both hunters and anti-hunters want to preserve wildlife, only hunters are doing something about it."

In the following viewpoint, Terry Anderson argues that hunting is good for wildlife conservation. Anderson provides examples from an African property turned wildlife ranch and farm. Anderson outlines successful principles and actions that made a difference in numbers of animal species and reduced illegal hunting by native people who instead became conservation managers. The author uses data from two African countries—one in which hunting was banned and the other in which it was allowed and practiced—to make his case that "hunting is the engine of profit that allows sustainable conservation. Anderson is Professor Emeritus at Montana State University and senior fellow at the Hoover Institution.

AS YOU READ, CONSIDER THE FOLLOWING QUESTIONS:

1. According to Anderson, how was elephant hunting by bushmen reduced?
2. What two examples from the viewpoint demonstrate how hunting is good for wildlife conservation?
3. As suggested by the author, what caused poaching in Kenya?

"How Hunting Saves Animals," by Terry Anderson, The Board of Trustees of Leland Stanford Junior University, October 29, 2015. ©2018 by the Board of Trustees of Leland Stanford Junior University. Reprinted by permission.

Some wildlife conservation properties allow licensed hunting in order to limit illegal hunting. The argument is, regulating hunting encourages conservation.

In 2013, the Dallas Safari Club worked with Namibian wildlife officials to auction a hunt of a black rhino, the most endangered of the rhino species. They expected to raise as much as $1 million from the auction with 100 percent of the proceeds going to rhino conservation efforts. Moreover, the rhino to be hunted was a cantankerous old bull, no longer of breeding age, which was harassing and even killing other rhinos.

Nonetheless, animal rights groups viciously attacked the Dallas Safari Club even to the point of threatening bodily harm to club leaders and anyone who bid on the hunt. Not surprisingly the auction brought far less than $1 million—$350,000. Further opposition from the animal rights groups pressured the US Fish and Wildlife Service to disallow importation of the trophy on the grounds that the Endangered Species Act protects endangered species even if they reside outside our borders. Finally, in 2015 the USFWS recanted and issued the importation permit, and the hunter bagged his rhino.

This raises the question: Is hunting good for wildlife conservation? To understand why the answer is unequivocally yes, consider the conservation story of Marty Anderson, a Hoover Institution board member.

Kenya banned hunting completely in 1977. The result of the ban is no better illustrated than on Galana Ranch, a property almost as large as Yellowstone Park. The Galana story is one that should be in every hunter's arsenal for responding to anti-hunters because it illustrates what hunting can do for wildlife and what happens when hunting is banned. (Details of this story can be found in *Galana: Elephants, Game Domestication, and Cattle on a Kenya Ranch*.) Leaving emotion aside, hunter-conservationists must continue to provide evidence, not rhetoric, that hunting is an environmentally sound practice—something that anti-hunting zealots rarely do. Through examples such a Galana, hunters can drive home the message that hunting is sustainable conservation.

We pick up the story of Galana Ranch in 1960 when Martin Anderson ventured to the Dark Continent on his first hunt. He was lured to Africa by the sights and sounds familiar to all who have read Hemingway or Ruark. But his hunting passion was quickly directed to wildlife conservation.

In 1960, Kenyan wildlife was abundant and its politics were turbulent. The Mau Mau Rebellion signaled the end of colonial rule, leading most colonialists to ask one another, "Have you sold your land yet?" As a retired Marine, lawyer, and entrepreneur, however, Anderson saw Kenya' s challenges as an opportunity.

Having whetted his appetite by investing in a 1,500-acre farm, Anderson took a giant leap into sustainable wildlife conservation when he bid on and won a 46-year lease on the 1.6 million acre Galana Ranch on the border with Tsavo East National Park.

As an astute businessman, financing the $100,000 winning bid and finding local management partners was not a problem. But Anderson had to ask himself. "Was developing this virgin land the right thing to do? Would we destroy it for the elephant and the Waliangulu [bushmen]?" Ultimately, he pursued a strategy which incorporated cattle ranching and hunting so as to generate income and preserve the conservation values.

Anderson and his partners developed pipelines, water points, roads, airstrips, and lodges, all of which contributed to the financial and conservation bottom lines. They generated revenues from 16,000 cattle and from hunting every species from the big five—rhino, elephants, Cape buffalo, lion, and leopard—to the smallest

duikers. Wherever possible, they employed native Kenyans in their cattle and wildlife operations.

One of the first management challenges on Galana was to find a way to reduce elephant hunting by bushmen. Although they hunted only with poison-tipped arrows launched from wooden longbows with 100 pound draw weights and only for meat (not ivory), the bushmen were so proficient that they were decimating the Dabassa elephant herd, which roamed Galana and Tsavo East. Anderson reported that one search "between the Galana and Tana Rivers, discovered the carcasses of about 900 elephants," including "352 tusks, weighting more than 6,500 pounds." Rather than trying to force them to stop killing elephants, Anderson incorporated the Waliangulu into his elephant management program, allowing them to cull elephants on a sustained yield basis.

For ten years, Galana made profits from safari hunting based on sound conservation principles. Anderson's success gives meaning to the old rancher adage, "If it pays, it stays."

Unfortunately, Anderson and the other Kenyan hunter-conservationists ultimately lost out to so-called animal "welfare" activists. In May of 1977, anti-hunters succeeded in banning all "legal" hunting in Kenya. Without hunting, wildlife on Galana ceased being an asset. Hunting had provided a major source of revenue for sustainable, profitable, private conservation. Thanks to the wildlife activists, though, there were no revenues and no hunters or guides in the field to police against poaching. Not surprisingly, poachers slaughtered more than 5,000 of the 6,000 elephants Anderson and his partners had conserved.

Perhaps more importantly, hunting provided native people with incomes and with meat, giving them an incentive to be part of the conservation effort. With wildlife all but gone, the government proposed in 2013 to put 1.2 million acres of the original ranch under irrigation, a project that will not be sustainable.

Anderson summarized the hunting/anti-hunting debate as follows: "Sadly, the often emotional rhetoric between the hunting and the non-hunting communities obscures a large area of shared agreement. Both camps want passionately to preserve animal populations. Both sides know that wildlife needs protection from a shrinking wildlife habitat and a growing human population." The difference is that Anderson and his hunting clients were actually making wildlife and its habitat a sustainable asset.

In 2006, I was invited to Kenya to participate in a conference debating whether to resurrect Kenyan hunting. One of the sponsors of the conference, IFAW (International Fund for Animal Welfare), packed the first rows of the auditorium with anti-hunting advocates. My role was to debate famed Richard Leakey, who was the director of the Kenya Wildlife Service when the hunting ban was implemented. Given his reputation and the sympathetic audience, I would have preferred facing a Cape buffalo with my bow as I had done a few years before. Leakey took the podium first as his allies listened intently. He opened saying "If anyone here thinks there is no hunting in Kenya, he is wrong. The 'hunting' is illegal hunting for bush meat, and it is decimating wildlife outside the protected areas."

The comparison of data between Kenya, where hunting was banned, and Botswana, where it was allowed until 2014, and the Galana story demonstrate that hunting is the engine of profit that allows sustainable conservation. The Kenyan elephant population fell precipitously between 1973 and 2013 while the Botswanan elephant population skyrocketed. Seizures of illegal ivory were nearly five time larger in Kenya than Botswana between 1989 and 2011. And Kenya accounted for more than 15 percent of all illegal ivory seizure in Africa over the past two decades compared to just over 3 percent for Botswana. These data show that the prohibition of hunting kills the goose that lays golden eggs for the people of Africa and for the wildlife.

With such evidence, you would think the debate would be over, but the anti-hunting groups claiming to represent "animal welfare" continue their rant. While it is true that both hunters and anti-hunters want to preserve wildlife, as Anderson said, only hunters are doing something about it, and they have the evidence to prove it.

EVALUATING THE AUTHOR'S ARGUMENTS:

Viewpoint author Terry Anderson writes that "both camps want passionately to preserve animal populations." Which individuals is Anderson referring to? Explain the stance of both sides, why each side thinks it is right, and the consequences of this as outlined by the author.

There Is No Rationale for Hunting in Developed Nations

"Hunters cause injuries, pain and suffering to animals who are not adapted to defend themselves from bullets, traps and other cruel killing devices."

In Defense of Animals

In the following viewpoint, In Defense of Animals argues that hunting is nothing short of killing, there are no gray areas. Hunting causes pain and suffering for animals, drives extinction, is unfair, and is definitely not about conservation. The author also maintains that animals are not crops to be harvested and that natural predators should be allowed to control wild animal populations. In Defense of Animals is an international organization working towards the protection of animals and the environment.

AS YOU READ, CONSIDER THE FOLLOWING QUESTIONS:

1. According to the author, why do wildlife agencies promote hunting?
2. Explain how two animal species mentioned suffer from sanctioned hunting.
3. Identify two ways to combat hunting at the state level, as stated in this viewpoint.

Do humans have a right to kill animals like lions in their natural habitat simply for sport?

Hunting may have played an important role, next to plant gathering and scavenging, for human survival in prehistoric times, but the vast majority of modern hunters in developed countries stalk and kill animals for recreation. Hunting is a violent and cowardly form of outdoor entertainment that kills hundreds of millions of animals every year, many of whom are wounded and die a slow and painful death.

Hunters cause injuries, pain and suffering to animals who are not adapted to defend themselves from bullets, traps and other cruel killing devices. Hunting destroys animal families and habitats, and leaves terrified and dependent baby animals behind to starve to death.

Because state wildlife agencies use hunting, trapping and fishing licenses as a source of income, today's wildlife management actively promotes the killing of wild animals, and joined by a powerful hunting lobby even sells wildlife trophy hunts to those who enjoy killing them. For instance, the California Department of Fish and Wildlife received $45,000 from the sale of a killing tag for California Desert Bighorn Sheep, sold at the 41st Safari Club International Convention in Reno, Nevada. Getting the trophy carcass is an unwritten guarantee.

Hunting Causes Pain and Suffering

A mere four percent of the human US population hunts, compared to 22 percent—over 70 million people—who enjoy watching wildlife alive. Wild animal watchers spend over $20 billion more than hunters on their activities that respect, rather than harm animals.

Despite increasing public opposition, hunting is permitted on 60 percent of US public lands, including in over 50% of wildlife refuges, many national forests and state parks; on federal land alone (more than half a billion acres), more than 200 million animals are killed every year (McCarthy).

Quick kills are rare, and many animals suffer prolonged, painful deaths when hunters severely injure but fail to kill them. Bow hunting exacerbates the problem, evidenced by dozens of scientific studies that have shown that bow hunting yields more than a 50 percent wounding and crippling rate. Some hunting groups promote shooting animals in the face or in the gut, which is a horrifically painful way to die.

Several states allow a spring bear hunt during the months when bears emerge from hibernation. These bears are not only still lethargic, which makes them easy targets for hunters, but many of the females are either pregnant or lactating. Mother bears are often shot while out and about foraging, while hiding their cubs in trees or leaving them in their dens. When mother bears are killed, their nursing cubs have little to no chance of survival as they will either starve or be killed by predators.

The stress that hunting inflicts on animals—the noise, the fear, and the constant chase—severely restricts their ability to eat adequately and store the fat and energy they need to survive the winter. Hunting also disrupts migration and hibernation, and the campfires, recreational vehicles and trash adversely affect both wildlife and the environment. For animals like wolves, who mate for life and have close-knit family units, hunting can destroy entire communities.

Hunting Is Not Sport

Hunting is often called a "sport," to disguise a cruel, needless killing spree as a socially acceptable activity. However, the concept of sport involves competition between two consenting parties, adherence to rules and fairness ensured by an intervening referee, and achieving highest scores but not death as the goal of the sporting events. In hunting, the animal is forced to "participate" in a live-or-die situation that always leads to the death of the animal, whereas the hunter leaves, their life never remotely at stake.

Hunting Is Not Fair Chase

Despite hunters' common claim of adhering to a "fair chase" code, there is no such thing. With an arsenal of rifles, shotguns, muzzle-loaders, handguns, bows and arrows, hunters kill more than 200 million animals yearly—and likely crippling, orphaning, and harassing millions more. The annual death toll in the US includes 42 million mourning doves, 30 million squirrels, 28 million quail, 25 million rabbits, 20 million pheasants, 14 million ducks, 6 million deer, and thousands of geese, bears, moose, elk, antelope, swans, cougars, turkeys, wolves, foxes, coyotes, bobcats, boars, and other woodland inhabitants. Hunters also frequently use food and electronic callers to lure unsuspecting animals in front of their weapons. The truth is, the animal, no matter how well-adapted to escaping natural predators she or he may be, has virtually no way to escape death once he or she is in the cross hairs of a scope mounted on a rifle or a crossbow.

Hunting Is Not Conservation

Wildlife management, population control and wildlife conservation are euphemisms for killing—hunting, trapping and fishing for fun. A percentage of the wild animal population is specifically mandated to be killed. Hunters want us to believe that killing animals equals population control equals conservation, when in fact hunting causes overpopulation of deer, the hunters' preferred victim species, destroys animal families, and leads to ecological disruption as well as skewed population dynamics.

Because state wildlife agencies are partly funded by hunters and other wildlife killers, programs are in place to manipulate habitat and artificially bolster "game" populations while ignoring "non-game" species. These programs lead to overpopulation and unbalanced ecosystems by favoring buck only hunts, pen-raising pheasants and other birds as living targets for hunters, transporting wild turkeys, raccoons and other species across state lines to boost populations for hunters and trappers to kill, and by exterminating predators such as wolves and mountain lions, in order to increase prey animals like elk and deer to then justify hunting as needed for "population control."

Hunting Contributes to Species Extinction

Hunting has contributed to the historical extinction of animal species all over the world, including the Southern Appalachian birds, the passenger pigeon and the Carolina parakeet (the only member of the parrot family native to the eastern United States), the eastern elk, the eastern cougar, the Tasmanian tiger and the great auk.

Wild Animals are Not Crops

Wildlife managers and hunters treat wild animals like a crop, of which a percentage can be "harvested" annually—to them, wild animals are no different than a field of wheat. This selective mis-management, with its exclusive focus on numbers to be killed, ignores the science that shows that nonhumans, just like humans, have similar capabilities to experience emotions, and have families and other social associations built on multi-leveled relationships.

Natural Carnivores are the Real Ecosystem Managers

While hunters and so-called wildlife professionals pretend to have control over ecosystems and the animals they kill, natural predators such as wolves, mountain lions and bears are the real ecosystem managers, if allowed to survive naturally. For instance, the reintroduction of wolves to Yellowstone National Park caused ripple effects throughout the ecosystem, with an increase in biodiversity, including a higher occurrence of beavers, several bird and plant species, and natural habitat and stream recovery.

What You Can Do

Join In Defense of Animals and support our efforts to end recreational hunting.

Before you support a wildlife or conservation group, ask about its position on hunting and trapping. Some groups, including the National Wildlife Federation, Defenders of Wildlife, the National Audubon Society, the Izaak Walton League, the Wilderness Society, and the World Wildlife Fund support recreational hunting, or they do not oppose it.

If you are a student of environmental studies, conservation and natural resource management or wildlife biology, challenge the concept of hunting as the foundation for wildlife conservation and management. Become familiar with non-lethal human/wildlife conflict solutions, and educate your classmates, your professors and your community.

Attend public meetings of your state's wildlife agency, voice your opinion against hunting in their public commenting process. Speak up, write letters and comments, and encourage others to do the same.

Join or form an anti-hunting organization and help spread the word about the injustice done against wild animals by hunters and state wildlife agencies.

Contact your state's governor and wildlife agency, and request equal consideration of non-hunters in employment opportunities, and equal representation of non-hunters in any decision-making process about wildlife.

EVALUATING THE AUTHOR'S ARGUMENTS:

In this viewpoint, In Defense of Animals clearly outlines a case against hunting. Compare and contrast the arguments in this viewpoint to the anti-hunting perspective of PETA in an earlier viewpoint.

Humans Are the Leading Cause of Animal Extinctions

"In just the past 40 years, nearly 52 percent of the planet's wildlife species have been eliminated."

World Animal Foundation

In the following viewpoint, the World Animal Foundation argues that human activities are bringing the world's animal populations to the brink of extinction. According to the author, legal hunting and illegal hunting, or poaching, are the cause. In addition to hunting, wild animals are in demand as exotic pets or as ingredients in bogus medicines, good luck charms, and wild meat. The World Animal Foundation is an organization dedicated to protecting and preserving animals.

AS YOU READ, CONSIDER THE FOLLOWING QUESTIONS:
1. What is poaching according to the author, and how does it cause extinction of animals?
2. Identify two animal species from the viewpoint article and explain why they are hunted.
3. Which animal identified by the author is a common pet?

"Hunting Wildlife to Extinction," World Animal Foundation. Reprinted by permission.

Once the most abundant of all rhino species, the black rhinoceros has becme endngered because of excessive poaching.

In just the past 40 years, nearly 52 percent of the planet's wildlife species have been eliminated. The leading cause of these shocking declines is irresponsible and unethical human activities. In addition to the devastating consequences of deforestation, animal agriculture, development, and environmental pollution, the wildlife trade is playing a major role in species extinction.

Poaching, which involves the illegal killing, hunting and capturing of wild animals for sale, is the biggest threat to wildlife after habitat destruction. Poaching is hunting without legal permission. The difference between poaching and hunting is the law.

Legal hunters also kill tens of millions of animals per year. For each of those animals, another animal is illegally killed. Whether done legally or illegally, all types of hunting have led to extinction of species. If not controlled, many more animals will be doomed to extinction.

In addition to their body parts, the animals themselves are in demand as exotic "pets." There are around 5,000 tigers being kept as pets in the US, while only around 3,000 remain in the wild. Australia's palm cockatoos, stolen from the wild, sell for tens of thousands of dollars on the black market.

Illegal wildlife trade generates up to 20 billion dollars each year, making it the fourth most lucrative illegal trade operation on the planet—just after drugs, human trafficking and the arms trade. The animals who fall victim to this trade are quickly becoming threatened and endangered. As their numbers drop, their value on the black market increases.

The rise in human population has been accompanied by rapid economic growth in some parts of the world. This growth has led to affluence and a huge and growing demand for animal by-products. China is now the largest importer of illegal wildlife. But poaching knows no boundaries. The United States is the second largest importer of illegal wildlife.

The exponential rise in illegal wildlife trade threatens to undo the decades of hard work by conservationists. Wildlife trade is now run by large international criminal syndicates with deep pockets and tentacles reaching into corrupt governments secretly abetting their activities. There are no available exact figures as to the size of this trade, but there are estimates that it could be as vast as $150 billion annually.

Iconic Species Being Hunted to Extinction

Some of the most common forms of poaching are the hunting and killing of elephants for their ivory, tigers for their skin and bones, and rhinoceros for the alleged medicinal value of their horns.

A huge surge in black market prices of ivory in China has led to heightened activity in elephant poaching in Africa. Over 30,000 elephants were killed in one year alone. The ban on ivory trade by virtually all African governments has done little to deter the poachers. In Tanzania, frenzied poaching has reduced the number of elephants from 100,000 in 2010 to just 44,000 presently. Poaching eliminated 48% of the elephant population in Mozambique during the last 5 to 6 years. Many of the local populace kill the animals for cash. Even militia groups are involved in the poaching of elephants.

The sub-Saharan black rhinoceros is now almost extinct by extensive poaching. There are only 4,000 of these animals left now, compared to the 100,000 that roamed the wilds not even half a century ago. An almost 7,700% rise in poaching of white and black rhinos has occurred in 9 years in South Africa.

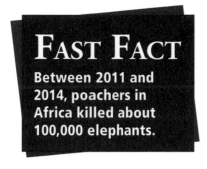

Rising affluence in Vietnam in the last decade has spiked the demand for rhino horns. Rhino horns are crushed into powdered form for its bogus medicinal value.

This is just one chapter of the sordid story. Millions of animals, birds, plants and marine life are killed every year. Wildlife trade accounts for the killing or capture of 100 million tons of fish, 1.5 million living birds, and almost 450,000 tons of plants annually. The combined population of all species of wildlife on Earth has fallen by as much as 40% since the 1970's.

Poaching Facts

- One rhino is poached every 8 hours. Rhino horns are more valuable than gold. They can sell for as much as $30,000 a pound. Gold is worth about $22,000 a pound. Rhino horns are believed to cure impotence, fever, hangovers, and even cancer, but they actually have no medicinal properties. Rhino horns are not true horns. They are an outgrowth of the skin, like human hair or fingernails. They have no more medicinal effect than chewing on your fingernails.
- Around 100 African elephants are killed every day by poachers—one elephant every 15 minutes. Ivory is carved into jewelry, trinkets, utensils, and figurines. Heavily armed militias and crime networks use ivory profits for terrorism and war funding.
- Asian elephants are also at risk. Only around 32,000 Asian elephants remain in the wild. Around 30 percent of the remaining population are inhumanely held prisoners in zoos, circuses, and roadside attractions for human entertainment and profit.

- Lemurs are among the most endangered mammals on Earth. 90% of all lemur species are considered vulnerable, endangered or critically endangered. Hunting lemurs for meat is diminishing their populations, already decimated by deforestation and climate changes.

- Logging, roads and migrations caused by wars have brought people within the habitats of gorillas. Subsistence hunting has quickly grown into an illicit commercial business of gorilla meat, served up as "bushmeat" to wealthy clientele. Gorillas are also killed for their body parts for folk remedies, and as "trophies." Baby gorillas are poached and sold for up to $40,000 each. Less than 900 mountain gorillas survive in Africa due to poaching.

- Musk deer populations in Afghanistan, Pakistan, Bhutan, India, Nepal and Myanmar have been nearly wiped out for their sacs that contain ingredients used in perfumes—despite a ban on musk from international trade.

- Tigers are poached for their teeth, claws, and whiskers, believed to provide good luck and protective powers. Skins and bones are considered status symbols. One tiger can bring as much as $50,000 on the black market.

- Up to half of Africa's lions have been illegally killed in just 20 years. Only about 32,000 remain in the wild.

- The sun bear as a species has been rendered almost extinct in its habitat in South-east Asia, Myanmar, Bangladesh and North-Eastern India. The gall bladders of these animals find use in medicines among the Chinese. A bear's gallbladder can fetch more than $3,000 in Asia.

- Poached sharks, manta rays, and sea cucumbers are used by Asian consumers to make shark fin soup. Over 11,000 sharks are killed every hour, every day.

- The American black bear is one of the top 10 most endangered bears on the planet. While 34 states have banned the trade of black bear bile and gallbladders, poaching and legal hunting is killing almost 50,000 bears every year. Their gallbladders and bile are sold to treat diseases of the heart, liver, and even diabetes.

- Over 28,000 freshwater turtles are poached daily—used for medicine, food and kept as pets. About 80 percent of Asia's freshwater turtle species are now in danger of extinction.
- The Sunda pangolin's population in its habitat in the jungles of Malaysia and Java, Indonesia has halved in the last fifteen years. Their meat fetches considerable demand as a luxury food among affluent Chinese, and their scales are sought for their medicinal properties.
- Millions of Tokay geckos are poached every year from Southeast Asia, the Philippines and Pacific islands for use in traditional medicine.
- Despite being on the US Fish and Wildlife Service's Endangered List since 1998, bighorn sheep populations continue to dwindle. Their antlers sell for over $20,000 on the black market.
- Poaching isn't limited to exotic and threatened species. Deer and other wildlife species are often hunted "out of season." Millions of animals are killed every year.

These are a few of many cases which have come to light, while many cases of over-exploitation of species have gone unnoticed. Conservation efforts, and various laws banning the illegal trade in wildlife resources, have had little effect in deterring those involved in wildlife trade. Educating humans on the urgent need to conserve our wildlife resources also seems to be falling on deaf ears. Until consumers stop purchasing wild animal products, and governments make the issue more of a priority, the wildlife trade will continue to flourish.

EVALUATING THE AUTHOR'S ARGUMENTS:

In this viewpoint, the World Animal Foundation examines the issues of poaching and illegal wildlife trade. Discuss and brainstorm ideas to effectively increase education efforts that would convince consumers not to buy animal products.

Hunting Revenue Contributes to Conservation Efforts

"Animal rights groups fail to recognize the value of hunting in conservation and even claim hunting is a leading threat to wildlife."

Joe Hosmer

In the following viewpoint, Joe Hosmer argues that wildlife actually benefits from hunting. Hosmer explains that, historically, hunters were the ones who initiated conservation efforts through harvest limits and other practices that resulted in the conservation and revival of certain species. They also drove legislation to impose fees on hunters and to funnel those fees back into wildlife conservation. This, the author contends, creates a value for wildlife. Hosmer is president of the Safari Club International Foundation, an organization which promotes the conservation of wildlife through the practice of sustainable use.

AS YOU READ, CONSIDER THE FOLLOWING QUESTIONS:

1. How does the North American Model of Wildlife Conservation affect wildlife populations?
2. According to the author, how is hunting beneficial to Africa?
3. What does the author mean when he explains that value must be created for wildlife?

Hunting is vital to the conservation and sustainable management of wildlife populations. Both the US Fish and Wildlife Service and the Convention on International Trade in Endangered Species recognize the importance of hunting in conservation and have special provisions in their regulations to ensure hunting continues. Animal rights and welfare activist groups fail to recognize the value of hunting in conservation and even claim hunting is a leading threat to wildlife. In fact, hunting remains a timeless tradition, a livelihood, and a necessity for conservation.

Does hunting really help animal conservation efforts?

Hunters pioneered sustainable wildlife management through the creation of North American Model of Wildlife Conservation. After early settlers diminished wildlife populations through unregulated harvesting, hunters and anglers assumed responsibility for the management of wildlife and worked to conserve species through harvest limits and the establishment of conservation organizations. Since its implementation in the 1860s, the North American Model has been responsible for the revival of multiple species, including white-tailed deer, elk, and black bears among others. Deer populations have grown to 32 million since the mid-1900s thanks to the North American Model, where science and sustainability are central. Research is conducted yearly to ensure that harvest is sustainable and adapted to meet the management goals set for the population size. Further, state conservation programs provide groundbreaking research into the most pressing issues facing wildlife management and rely heavily on revenue generated by hunters to remain at the forefront of those issues.

Through legislation such as the Federal Aid in Wildlife Restoration Act, better-known as the Pittman-Robertson Act, excise taxes and fees paid by hunters are directed to restoration programs to be used exclusively by state fish and wildlife agencies. The revenue from an 11 percent tax on long guns, for example, is distributed nationwide and assists with conservation research and project funding. Last year, the US Department of the Interior announced that $1.1 billion of excise tax revenue paid by sportsmen and sportswomen would go toward funding state conservation and recreation projects. Programs like Pittman-Robertson and personal donations to conservation organizations allow sportsmen and sportswomen to contribute billions to conservation annually. In 2011, North American hunters spent $38.3 billion with $3 billion directed exclusively to conservation initiatives. These efforts are the foundation of the conservation funding system.

The practice of funding conservation programs through hunting revenue is not only applicable to North America, but has been shown to be effective internationally. As in the US, hunting revenue from the sale of licenses and tags in Africa and Asia also goes directly to funding wildlife management and other conservation efforts. Many African countries rely on tourism for economic stability; one of the highest grossing forms of tourism in Africa is hunting. Hunting tourism means jobs to local peoples of Africa. According to a 2004 study, in Tanzania hunting tourism employed approximately 3,700 people annually. In turn, those workers supported 88,240 family members.

Many wildlife organizations recognize the benefits hunting tourism brings to African communities. A recent World Wildlife Fund community-based natural resources management report states that the economic benefits of hunting "quickly reinforce the value of a conservancy's wildlife resource and such community awareness is a powerful anti-poaching stimulus, creating effective internal social pressures against the illegal harvesting of game."

Creating value for wildlife is a key aspect in ensuring wildlife survival and that is exactly what the presence of hunting accomplishes. Habitat loss and human-wildlife conflict are growing threats to wildlife populations. This is due to land-use change for various human purposes, such as agriculture. As long as wildlife attack livestock and eat or trample crops, local people will continue to indiscriminately kill intruders that they perceive as a threat to their livelihood.

Scientifically based, regulated hunting provides value to wildlife for these local communities by showing the profits that can be generated by the legal harvest of a single animal. It is also conducive in creating socially acceptable population numbers, which ultimately decreases the possibility of wildlife conflict and therefore decreases the number of retaliatory killings, further conserving species.

Many opponents of the hunting industry ask: "If hunters love wildlife, why not donate the money instead of using it for hunting?" But no one asks a marathon runner to only write a check instead of actually running in a breast cancer awareness race. It is commonly understood that providing an opportunity for a person to contribute to a cause, while participating in something they love, increases the likelihood that a person will continue to contribute in the future.

Hunters respect wildlife and seek to conserve the wildlife that they hunt to ensure sustainable populations for the future. It is a lucrative form of tourism that not only creates value for wildlife, but also supports conservation programs, feeds local communities, provides jobs, and funds anti-poaching efforts. And, hunters also write checks for conservation, in addition to hunting.

Hunting is indisputably an effective form of conservation recognized by governments and wildlife organizations throughout the world. It generates revenue and provides tremendous opportunities for communities reliant on wildlife. Science dictates harvest numbers and research showcases its positive effects. Year after year, sportsmen and sportswomen demonstrate their impactful role in conservation and their efforts should not be stifled by the futile emotional arguments of those who harbor a moral grudge against the hunting industry.

EVALUATING THE AUTHOR'S ARGUMENTS:

In this viewpoint, Joe Hosmer writes that the anti-hunting establishment engages in "futile emotional arguments."
Is this the part of the same argument that Terry Anderson writes about in a previous viewpoint? Compare the points made about this theme from both viewpoints.

Viewpoint 6

There Is No Need to Harm Animals

"Hunting animals for food constitutes the infliction of violence and death on animals we have no need to harm at all."

Ashley Capps

In the following viewpoint, Ashley Capps attacks the supposition that some hunters use to justify their hunting habits. Capps argues that in the western world, people do not need to hunt and kill animals in order to provide their families with protein, as many hunters would say to justify their actions. The author also disputes another common argument from hunters, which contends that animal populations will exponentially increase without the culling effect of hunting. Capps writes, edits, and researches topics concerned with the welfare of farm animals and the vegan lifestyle.

AS YOU READ, CONSIDER THE FOLLOWING QUESTIONS:

1. According to Capps, what foods could people buy to replace protein from animals?
2. How does hunting drain family resources, as stated by the author?
3. As defined in the viewpoint, what is "reverse evolution?"

"Hunting for Wildlife Population Control and Ethical Eating?" by Ashley Capps, Free From Harm, January 14, 2015. Reprinted by permission.

Some animal rights advocates believe that, with all of the dietary options available to modern humans, it's not necessary to eat animals at all—whether hunted or farmed.

We not infrequently hear from hunters who make the case that while factory farming is wrong, there is nothing unethical about eating animals who have been hunted in the wild. After all, the reasoning goes, the animals live a completely natural life just as nature intended, and, according to hunters, generally die more quickly, and with less fear and pain, than they would experience with other predators.

But all of this begs the question of necessity. Most North Americans and Europeans (and many others) who hunt do not do so because they have to in order to survive. Most of these hunters shop at grocery stores for at least some portion of their food, stores where they have access to dried beans, nuts, grains, produce and other nutritious plant proteins. In such cases, hunting animals for food is unnecessary, and, like farming animals, constitutes the infliction of violence and death on animals we have no need to harm at all.

As Brian Luke writes in *Brutal: Manhood and the Exploitation of Animals,*

North American men do not hunt out of necessity; they typically do not hunt to protect people or animals, nor to keep themselves or their families from going hungry. Rather, they pursue hunting for its own sake, as a sport. This point is obscured by the fact that many hunters consume the flesh of their kills with their families, thus giving the appearance that hunting is a subsistence tactic. A close reading of the hunting literature, however, reveals that hunters eat the flesh of their kills as an ex post facto attempt at morally legitimating an activity they pursue for its own sake. The hunter often portrays himself as providing for his family through a successful kill and "harvest." This posture seeks to ritually reestablish a stereotypical masculine provider role less available now than may once have been. In reality hunting today is typically not a source of provision but actually drains family resources. Deer hunters, for example, spend on average twenty dollars per pound of venison, once all the costs of equipment, licenses, transportation, unsuccessful hunts, and so forth are calculated.

Then there is the defense that hunting animals is necessary to wildlife "population control." This argument is especially common as a justification for hunting deer. But as Doris Lin writes in, *What Will Happen to Animals If Everyone Goes Vegan?*

> *Hunters sometimes argue that if they were to stop hunting, the deer population would explode. This is a false argument, because if hunting were to stop, we would also stop the practices that increase the deer population. State wildlife management agencies artificially boost the deer population in order to increase recreational hunting opportunities for hunters. By clearcutting forests, planting deer-preferred plants and requiring tenant farmers to leave a certain amount of their crops unharvested in order to feed the deer, the agencies*

are creating the edge habitat that is preferred by deer and also feeding the deer. If we stop hunting, we would also stop these tactics that increase the deer population.

If we stopped hunting, we would also stop breeding animals in captivity for hunters. Many nonhunters are unaware of state and private programs that breed quail, partridges and pheasants in captivity, for the purpose of releasing them in the wild, to be hunted.

And in *Scientific Arguments Against Hunting*, Lin writes,

Big "game" animals like white-tailed deer and black bears rarely exceed their biological carrying capacity—the maximum number of individuals the ecosystem will support without threatening other species. If they exceed that number, a lack of food will kill the weakest individuals, and will also cause the pregnant females to resorb embryos and have fewer offspring. The strongest will survive and the population will become healthier.

Unlike nature, hunters select the small and the weak to survive—reverse evolution. Instead of targeting the young, old, or sick individuals, hunters kill the largest, strongest males. Because hunters prefer large males with big horns, bighorn sheep in Alberta, Canada are now smaller, with smaller horns, compared to thirty years ago. And because hunters prefer to kill elephants with tusks, the African and Asian elephants that have a genetic mutation that leaves them tuskless are now dominating those populations.

EVALUATING THE AUTHOR'S ARGUMENTS:

In this viewpoint, Ashley Capps writes about animals that are being bred in captivity for the sake of hunters and hunting. How does this compare to farming and raising of livestock?

Chapter 3

What Is the Future of Hunting?

Will hunting for sport gradually become an activity of the past?

Without Conservation Efforts Species Extinction Is a Threat

Barry Yeoman

"The bird was hunted out of existence, victimized by the fallacy that no amount of exploitation could endanger a creature so abundant."

In the following excerpted viewpoint, Barry Yeoman argues that even the most robust wildlife species can become extinct if humans are allowed to hunt and kill animals in that species with abandon. Yeoman uses the case of the passenger pigeon, a species once so abundant in North America that traveling flocks would block out the sun in the sky, to illustrate that conservation efforts are needed for even the most common and plentiful of wildlife. The passenger pigeon became extinct precisely because humans assumed the species was so abundant that no amount of hunting could make a dent in the population. Yeoman is an award-winning journalist whose work has appeared in *Audubon*, *The Washington Post*, *The Nation*, and *New Republic*, among others.

In May 1850, a 20-year-old Potawatomi tribal leader named Simon Pokagon was camping at the headwaters of Michigan's Manistee River during trapping season when a far-off gurgling sound startled him. It seemed as if "an army of horses laden with sleigh bells was advancing through the deep forests towards me," he later wrote. "As I listened more intently, I concluded that instead of the tramping of horses it was distant thunder; and yet the morning was clear, calm, and beautiful." The mysterious sound came "nearer and nearer," until Pokagon deduced its source: "While I gazed in wonder and astonishment, I beheld moving toward me in an unbroken front millions of pigeons, the first I had seen that season."

These were passenger pigeons, *Ectopistes migratorius*, at the time the most abundant bird in North America and possibly the world. Throughout the 19th century, witnesses had described similar sightings of pigeon migrations: how they took hours to pass over a single spot, darkening the firmament and rendering normal conversation inaudible. Pokagon remembered how sometimes a traveling flock, arriving at a deep valley, would "pour its living mass" hundreds of feet into a downward plunge. "I have stood by the grandest waterfall of America," he wrote, "yet never have my astonishment, wonder, and admiration been so stirred as when I have witnessed these birds drop from their course like meteors from heaven."

Pokagon recorded these memories in 1895, more than four decades after his Manistee River observation. By then he was in the final years of his life. Passenger pigeons, too, were in their final years. In 1871 their great communal nesting sites had covered 850 square miles of Wisconsin's sandy oak barrens—136 million breeding adults, naturalist A.W. Schorger later estimated. After that the population plummeted until, by the mid-1890s, wild flock sizes numbered in

The once-common passenger pigeon was taken for granted and eventually hunted to extinction more than 100 years ago.

the dozens rather than the hundreds of millions (or even billions). Then they disappeared altogether, except for three captive breeding flocks spread across the Midwest. About September 1, 1914, the last known passenger pigeon, a female named Martha, died at the Cincinnati Zoo. She was roughly 29 years old, with a palsy that made her tremble. Not once in her life had she laid a fertile egg.

This year marks the 100th anniversary of the passenger pigeon's extinction. In the intervening years, researchers have agreed that the bird was hunted out of existence, victimized by the fallacy that no amount of exploitation could endanger a creature so abundant. Between now and the end of the year, bird groups and museums will commemorate the centenary in a series of conferences, lectures, and exhibits. Most prominent among them is Project Passenger Pigeon, a wide-ranging effort by a group of scientists, artists, museum curators, and other bird lovers. While their focus is on public education, an unrelated organization called Revive & Restore is attempting something far more ambitious and controversial: using genetics to bring the bird back.

Project Passenger Pigeon's leaders hope that by sharing the pigeon's story, they can impress upon adults and children alike our critical role in environmental conservation. "It's surprising to me how many educated people I talk to who are completely unaware that the passenger pigeon even existed," says ecologist David Blockstein, senior scientist at the National Council for Science and the Environment. "Using the centenary is a way to contemplate questions like, 'How was it possible that this extinction happened?' and 'What does it say about contemporary issues like climate change?'"

They Were Evolutionary Geniuses

Traveling in fast, gargantuan flocks throughout the eastern and midwestern United States and Canada—the males slate-blue with copper undersides and hints of purple, the females more muted—passenger pigeons would search out bumper crops of acorns and beechnuts. These they would devour, using their sheer numbers to ward off enemies, a strategy known as "predator satiation." They would also outcompete other nut lovers—not only wild animals but also domestic pigs that had been set loose by farmers to forage.

In forest and city alike, an arriving flock was a spectacle—"a feathered tempest," in the words of conservationist Aldo Leopold. One 1855 account from Columbus, Ohio, described a "growing cloud" that blotted out the sun as it advanced toward the city. "Children screamed and ran for home," it said. "Women gathered their long skirts and hurried for the shelter of stores. Horses bolted. A few people mumbled frightened words about the approach of the millennium, and several dropped on their knees and prayed." When the flock had passed over, two hours later, "the town looked ghostly in the now-bright sunlight that illuminated a world plated with pigeon ejecta."

Nesting birds took over whole forests, forming what John James Audubon in 1831 called "solid masses as large as hogs-heads." Observers reported trees crammed with dozens of nests apiece, collectively weighing so much that branches would snap off and trunks would topple. In 1871 some hunters coming upon the morning exodus of adult males were so overwhelmed by the sound and spectacle that some of them dropped their guns. "Imagine a thousand threshing machines running under full headway, accompanied by as many steamboats groaning off steam, with an equal quota of R.R. trains passing through covered bridges—imagine these massed into a single flock, and you possibly have a faint conception of the terrific roar," the *Commonwealth*, a newspaper in Fond du Lac, Wisconsin, reported of that encounter.

The birds weren't just noisy. They were tasty, too, and their arrival guaranteed an abundance of free protein. "You think about this especially with the spring flocks," says Blockstein, the ecologist. "The people on the frontiers have survived the winter. They've been eating whatever food they've been able to preserve from the year before. Then, all of a sudden, here's all this fresh meat flying by you. It must have been a time for great rejoicing: The pigeons are here!" (Not everyone shouted with joy. The birds also devoured crops, frustrating farmers and prompting Baron de Lahontan, a French soldier who explored North America during the 17th century, to write that "the Bishop has been forc'd to excommunicate 'em oftner than once, upon the account of the Damage they do to the Product of the Earth.")

The flocks were so thick that hunting was easy—even waving a pole at the low-flying birds would kill some. Still, harvesting for subsistence didn't threaten the species' survival. But after the Civil War came two technological developments that set in motion the pigeon's extinction: the national expansions of the telegraph and the railroad. They enabled a commercial pigeon industry to blossom, fueled by professional sportsmen who could learn quickly about new nestings and follow the flocks around the continent. "Hardly a train arrives that does not bring hunters or trappers," reported Wisconsin's *Kilbourn City Mirror* in 1871. "Hotels are full, coopers are busy making barrels, and men, women, and children are active in packing the birds or filling the barrels. They are shipped to all places on the railroad, and to Milwaukee, Chicago, St. Louis, Cincinnati, Philadelphia, New York, and Boston."

The professionals and amateurs together outflocked their quarry with brute force. They shot the pigeons and trapped them with nets, torched their roosts, and asphyxiated them with burning sulfur. They attacked the birds with rakes, pitchforks, and potatoes. They poisoned them with whiskey-soaked corn. Learning of some of these methods, Potawatomi leader Pokagon despaired. "These outlaws to all moral sense would touch a lighted match to the bark of the tree at the base, when with a flash—more like an explosion—the blast would reach every limb of the tree," he wrote of an 1880 massacre, describing how the scorched adults would flee and the squabs would "burst open upon hitting the ground." Witnessing this, Pokagon wondered what type of divine punishment might be "awaiting our white neighbors who have so wantonly butchered and driven from our forests these wild pigeons, the most beautiful flowers of the animal creation of North America."

Ultimately, the pigeons' survival strategy—flying in huge predator-proof flocks—proved their undoing. "If you're unfortunate enough to be a species that concentrates in time and space, you make yourself very, very vulnerable," says Stanley Temple, a professor emeritus of conservation at the University of Wisconsin.

Passenger pigeons might have even survived the commercial slaughter if hunters weren't also disrupting their nesting grounds—killing some adults, driving away others, and harvesting the squabs. "It was the double whammy," says Temple. "It was the demographic nightmare of overkill and impaired reproduction. If you're killing a species far faster than they can reproduce, the end is a mathematical certainty." The last known hunting victim was "Buttons," a female, which was shot in Pike County, Ohio, in 1900 and mounted by the sheriff's wife (who used two buttons in lieu of glass eyes). Almost seven decades later a man named Press Clay Southworth took responsibility for shooting Buttons, not knowing her species, when he was a boy.

Even as the pigeons' numbers crashed, "there was virtually no effort to save them," says Joel Greenberg, a research associate with Chicago's Peggy Notebaert Nature Museum and the Field Museum. "People just slaughtered them more intensely. They killed them until the very end."

Contemporary Environmentalism Arrived Too Late to Prevent the Passenger Pigeon's Demise

But the two phenomena share a historical connection. "The extinction was part of the motivation for the birth of modern 20th century conservation," says Temple. In 1900, even before Martha's death in the Cincinnati Zoo, Republican Congressman John F. Lacey of Iowa introduced the nation's first wildlife-protection law, which banned the interstate shipping of unlawfully killed game. "The wild pigeon, formerly in flocks of millions, has entirely disappeared from the face of the earth," Lacey said on the House floor. "We have given an awful exhibition of slaughter and destruction, which may serve as a warning to all mankind. Let us now give an example of wise conservation of what remains of the gifts of nature." That year Congress passed the Lacey Act, followed by the tougher Weeks-McLean Act in 1913 and, five years later, the Migratory Bird Treaty Act, which protected not just birds but also their eggs, nests, and feathers.

[…]

EVALUATING THE AUTHOR'S ARGUMENTS:

Viewpoint author Barry Yeoman uses a historical lesson to warn readers about threats to wildlife species today. Do you think this is an effective way to make a case?

Hunting Makes Sense for Controlling Invasive Species

"Experience has left a strong impression of insidiously multiplying snakes coincident with the disappearance of everything else."

Liza Lester

In the following viewpoint, Liza Lester analyzes the problem surrounding an explosion of an invasive species in the Florida Everglades. Burmese pythons have been imported to the United States as pets for some time, and in Florida people have been releasing them in the Everglades. The author maintains that although park personnel have been killing a lot more of the snakes recently, populations of native wildlife are suffering from the exotic invaders. Lester holds a doctorate in molecular and cellular biology and is Communications Officer for the Ecological Society of America.

AS YOU READ, CONSIDER THE FOLLOWING QUESTIONS:

1. According to the author, how did Burmese pythons get introduced to the Florida Everglades?
2. What native animals are disappearing from the Everglades as reported in the viewpoint?
3. Lester presents evidence about the python problem. Identify and explain two pieces of evidence.

Should the hunting of the overpopulated Burmese python, which is destroying native species, be permitted in the Everglades?

A waxing population of Burmese pythons has suspiciously paralleled waning sightings of native critters in Florida's Everglades, says a paper out this week in the *Proceedings of the National Academy of Sciences*. Following on the tail of an announcement two weeks ago (Jan 17th) that the US will ban imports and interstate sales of the exotic python and three other large constrictor snakes (yellow anacondas and northern and southern African pythons), the story has been attracting plenty of media attention.

The case against the python is not a slam dunk, but the authors amass circumstantial evidence of its guilt in connection to the missing native fauna, and legislators are buying it.

Burmese pythons (*Python molurus bivittatus*) are native to the warm latitudes of Southeast Asia, and arrived in Florida as pets. The python has an eclectic appetite, dining on more than forty varieties of evergladian mammal, bird and reptile, including other carnivores, endangered species, and the occasional alligator. Visitors and rangers have sighted pythons in the park for thirty years, but the park only began to view them as a resident population in 2000. A short decade later, the python had risen to the disreputable distinction of "conditional reptile," and was officially blacklisted.

Hopes that the cold winter of 2010 would kill off the pythons have been disappointed, as Terence explains in Tuesday's EcoTone post. In July 2010, Florida Fish and Wildlife forbade acquisition of new pythons, required grandfathered owners to microchip their pets and obtain a license, and instituted a permitting system for civilian python hunting in the public parks.

The US has imported 112,000 Burmese pythons since 1990, according to the US Fish and Wildlife Service. Owners have been known to release their sinuous darlings after the snakes, which can reach almost 20 feet, grow too large to cohabitate comfortably in the house. But park managers speculate that the 1992 category 5 storm Hurricane Andrew may be the primary source of the python population explosion. An internal Fish and Wildlife study found little genetic variation in the python population—a sign of a small, closely related foundling group.

"At least one facility had over 900 Burmese pythons at the time and was destroyed completely. This facility was within just a mile or so of what is believed to be the epicenter of the population, and it possessed animals from the same genetic origin. Since 1992 the FWC has put into place more stringent regulations on housing, disaster protocols and bio security in general," wrote Florida herpetologist Shawn Heflick in a lengthy and interesting Q&A accompanying PBS' Nature episode "Invasion of the Giant Pythons" in February 2010.

The python's success in its new home has bumped it from rare feral pet to alarming invasive species in the eyes of the managers responsible for the restoration of the Everglades. They don't know exactly how many snakes are in the park, but they know that they have been killing a lot more snakes lately.

"All of the pythons that are captured in the park are actually removed from the park, so that precludes us from doing mark-recapture studies," said lead author Michael Dorcas, in an interview with *The Atlantic*'s Brian Resnick. Since park policy is to dispose of the invasive snake, the researchers do not have unassailable data on the python's demographics. Their evidence of a population boom is a recorded surge in

FAST FACT

Over 2,000 pythons have been removed from Everglades National Park since 2002.

the number of snakes removed by rangers, which is not, as they say "corrected for effort," or for rangers' sensitivity to the presence of the python. Their data on the python's prey are similarly freighted.

The park service tracked road kill (of the fuzzy variety) in the Everglades from 1993 to 1999, with more systematic surveys of encounters with wildlife, both alive and dead, along Park roads from 1996-1997, and (at different intervals) from 2003 to 2010. They don't have truly methodical estimates of how many animals live in the swamp, or where rabbits and foxes and bobcats particularly like to hang out, but they have managed to quantify their every-day on-the-job experiences with wildlife in the park. Experience has left a strong impression of insidiously multiplying snakes coincident with the disappearance of everything else.

Between 1993 and 1999, over 250 raccoons died at the wheels of vehicles on the everglades' sparsely used roads. In the 80s, 'coons showed up so often in campgrounds that they were deemed a nuisance, and the park instituted unspecified control measures. Raccoon encounters have fallen by 89% since the 90s, fox by 83%, and deer by 89%. Rabbits seem to have vanished in the python high-traffic zone. The authors note that human encounters with other animals are more frequent where pythons are rare. The constellation of indirect evidence adds up strong suspicion of a python connection.

To boost their case that the rising tide of pythons is the variable responsible for the ebb in mammalian road deaths (and other encounters) the authors argue that disease and human influence are unlikely competing hypotheses. A single infectious agent is unlikely to take out such an evolutionarily broad swath of animals, and hunting in the park is already forbidden, they say.

Andrew Wyatt, president of the United States Association of Reptile Keepers was quick to point out the study's weaknesses on NPR's *Diane Rehm Show* on Wednesday. "The press and the media got quite carried away with the press release and actually reported a number of things that are not detailed in the paper at all," he said. "In the paper, there is no direct causation linked to the Burmese python, it's speculative. There are numerous studies out there that have been done in regards to mammal declines, and bird declines, in the Everglades that are linked back not to the Burmese python, but back to hydrology and high levels of mercury."

Wayne Pacelle, President and C.E.O. of the Humane Society of the United States, partially proved Wyatt's point with his rebuttal, overstating the decline in observations of mammals as direct measurements of disappearing animal populations, and ascribing the loss to Burmese pythons.

Demonstrating causation, if it is true, may be rather difficult. But what we have here is good preliminary data, a very strong itchy intuition, that something is not right in the swamp.

EVALUATING THE AUTHOR'S ARGUMENTS:

In this viewpoint, Liza Lester presents a case for the positive use of hunting. Using the author's viewpoint as a starting point, make your own case for the use of hunting when dealing with an invasive animal species.

Tribal Societies Must Be Allowed to Hunt

"The animals and everything that I have eaten from the land has moulded me, it has shaped me."

Survival International

In the following viewpoint, Survival International argues that hunting must continue as a way of life for tribal societies. Survival International provides examples that demonstrate how tribal societies depend on hunting and how the identities of individual tribe members are interconnected with hunting the animals inherent to native cultures. Survival International is a global organization that helps tribal people protect their lands, determine their futures, and defend their lives.

AS YOU READ, CONSIDER THE FOLLOWING QUESTIONS:
1. According to the authors, what natural resources often shape tribal society members?
2. When do tribal members resort to poaching, as stated by the authors?
3. Give two examples of what happens when tribal societies are denied traditionally hunted animals, as noted in the viewpoint.

"Hunting," Survival International. Reprinted by permission.

Certain tribal societies depend on hunting for survival. Connection to the land and nature is a big part of their culture.

Some tribes identify themselves as hunters of specific species. The Khanty of Siberia are reindeer hunters.

They use reindeer skins for clothing and shelter, meat for food and bones for knife handles. Their connection to the reindeer is vitally important to them as a people.

A Nenet reindeer herder in Siberia, Jakov Japtik, said "The snow is melting sooner, quicker and faster than before. The changes aren't good for the reindeer and ultimately what is good for the reindeer is good for us."

Many tribal societies have totem animals with which they have a kinship and which they do not hunt. Other species are hunted specifically for ceremonial, health or spiritual reasons.

This connection to specific animals has often resulted in tribes carefully protecting their environment to ensure that there is a plentiful supply of the animals that they depend upon.

Elder Whitehead Moose, of the Pikangikum tribe in Canada, said "Everything that you see in me, it is the land that has moulded me. The fish have moulded me. The animals and everything that I have eaten from the land has moulded me, it has shaped me. I believe every Aboriginal person has been moulded in this way."

In the face of outside pressures, such as influxes of settlers, "development" projects such as dams and oil exploration and the increasing risk of climate change, this fundamental relationship comes under threat.

A Khanty hunter said, "This is the only place where the land is clean in this region, we must keep this territory clean because if an oil company comes then we won't be able to hunt and keep reindeer, it will be the end."

"Don't They All Use Machine Guns Now?"

Myths about tribal people and hunting abound. British parliamentarian, Baroness Tonge, for example, claimed that Kalahari Bushmen were hunting using guns and 4×4 vehicles. But government officials have admitted that the Bushmen do not hunt with guns and there is no evidence that their hunting is unsustainable.

Hunting by tribal peoples on their own land has been severely restricted in many countries without evidence that they are reducing the populations of the animals they hunt.

The Hadza of Tanzania nearly lost their hunting rights to a safari hunting company.

Controlled hunting for profit is often more acceptable to governments than hunting by tribal peoples for their own needs.

When they are banned from their land by safari hunting companies or thrown off their land by settlers or ranchers, the impacts are severe. Tribal people are accused of "poaching" because they hunt their food. And they face arrest and beatings, torture and death, while fee-paying big game hunters are encouraged.

The Impact of Outlawing Hunting

Conservation areas, such as national parks, and conservation regulations in many countries outlaw hunting of specific species and in particular areas, usually without consulting the tribal communities who will be most affected.

In January 2010, the Canadian government banned caribou hunting in an area where Dene tribal people harvest around 6,000 caribou a year to feed their families.

Alternative sources of protein and iron are both more fatty and more expensive. Diabetes is a major problem among the Dene, who have already suffered due to forced evictions from their homelands.

Illa Bussidor, a Sayisi Dene, said "My dad was standing by the window. I saw that he was crying. 'I was a proud man,' he said. 'I hunted, and trapped for my family. I was so proud. But today my little girl brings home food from the garbage dump so I can eat.'"

Hunting "Charismatic" Creatures

Where the issue of indigenous hunting becomes particularly contentious is regarding species that are considered special, such as polar bears, seals and whales.

To many Arctic peoples, hunting these creatures is an integral part of their culture.

Charles Johnson, an Alaskan Inuit, said, "When I was a child, it was forbidden to speak our language, to do things like dancing because missionaries said we were worshipping the devils.

"We need to keep our traditions alive. That includes regaining our language, regaining our culture and polar bear hunting is part of that."

EVALUATING THE AUTHOR'S ARGUMENTS:

In this viewpoint, Survival International reports on the cultural aspects of hunting in tribal societies. Should tribal societies be allowed to hunt in all instances? Support your position, either for or against, with evidence from the viewpoint article.

Eco-tourism Should Replace Trophy Hunting

Teresa M. Telecky

"Animals like elephants and lions are much more valuable alive than dead, to the economies of African nations and to the entire world."

In the following viewpoint, Teresa M. Telecky argues against trophy hunting. The author exposes the link between trophy hunting and government corruption, especially in certain African countries. Telecky exposes the killing sprees that trophy hunters engage in, especially those in pursuit of trophies offered by certain hunting clubs, and suggests an alternative that emphasizes conservation. Telecky is a PhD zoologist and Vice President in the Wildlife Department for Humane Society International.

AS YOU READ, CONSIDER THE FOLLOWING QUESTIONS:

1. What big five African animals are pursued by trophy hunters, as reported by the author?
2. According to Telecky, how does corruption affect trophy hunting?
3. How can animals be more valuable alive than dead according to this viewpoint?

"Hunting Is a Setback to Wildlife Conservation," by Teresa M. Telecky, Earth Island Institute. This debate originally appeared in the Summer 2014 issue of *Earth Island Journal*. Reprinted by permission.

Among other benefits, willdlife watching allows local communities to become involved in conservation and to share that with tourists.

Nearly 40 years ago, Kenya banned trophy hunting. Within the past two years, other African countries have realized the wisdom of Kenya's approach and instituted similar bans. Botswana and Zambia, once major destinations for pursuers of Africa's "Big Five"—African elephant, African lion, Cape buffalo, leopard, and rhinoceros—have also prohibited this biologically reckless activity because of the harm it causes to wildlife populations. Even the United States, home to the world's largest number of trophy hunters, has taken steps to join the trend. In April, the US Fish and Wildlife Service (FWS) banned the import of sport-hunted elephant trophies from Zimbabwe and Tanzania over concerns that the hunts were driving down elephant populations already severely impacted by poachers.

It's about time. If the Dallas Safari Club auction for the opportunity to kill a critically endangered black rhino in Namibia proved anything, it is that trophy-seekers will pay an exorbitant amount of money for bragging rights and a head to hang on the wall, instead of using that wealth to preserve and protect wildlife.

The winner of the auction agreed to pay $350,000 for the right to kill the black rhino—a creature highly desired by those who seek to add the rarest animals to their trophy collections. Contemplate for a moment what money like that could buy in poor countries that are often riddled with corruption. According to Transparency International, Zimbabwe, Zambia, and Tanzania are three of the most corrupt countries in the world, and money from trophy-hunters fuels this corruption. Corrupt officials allow animals to be killed in dangerously high numbers—to the point of harming the conservation of the species. Corruption that led to poor wildlife management is exactly the reason that Kenya banned hunting so long ago and why others are following Kenya's lead today.

The Namibian government decided to allow the slaughter of a black rhino as a fundraising mechanism, but those funds will not necessarily go back to black rhino conservation as some claim. Instead, they will go into a general pot of money allocated to all manner of projects including those that have nothing to do with rhinos, or which could even be harmful to rhinos, such as "rural development."

Cashing in on the desires of some to shoot rare species and display their remains back home in lavish "trophy rooms"—macabre mausoleums filled with dead animals—is what is driving Namibia's approach, not the conservation needs of the species. The best way to conserve critically endangered species like the black rhino is to ensure that every animal remains alive and contributing to the genetic diversity of the species. Species with a diverse gene pool are more able to overcome challenges to their survival. The Namibian case proves, once again, that cold, hard cash undermines wildlife conservation.

Fortunately, the black rhino is listed as an endangered species under the US Endangered Species Act (ESA), meaning that the winner will need to get an import permit from the FWS to bring the carcass home. The ESA makes it clear that such permits should be granted only when the import will enhance the survival of the species in the wild. Once the winner applies for the import permit, there will be a 30-day comment period. We plan to provide evidence to the FWS that the recreational shooting of a member of a critically endangered species is harmful to that species. We invite you to sign a petition that we will submit along with our comments showing that people do not support issuance of the import permit.

The US government needs to understand that the American public does not support the Orwellian idea of killing endangered species to save them—even if it comes with a big cash payout. Where will it end? Will a Safari Club International member offer $1 million for the opportunity to shoot an orangutan, $2 million for an Asian elephant, and maybe even more for a Siberian tiger?

While those animals are highly protected because they are listed as endangered under the ESA, others are not so fortunate, and the numbers killed by American trophy hunters annually are staggering. In 2012, the parts of approximately 600 African elephants, 750 African lions, and 698 leopards were imported into this country.

American trophy hunters belong to clubs, such as the Dallas Safari Club and Safari Club International, where they can compete to kill the most animals for the most awards. To earn every award that SCI offers, at least 171 different animals from around the world must be killed. Many SCI members have records for killing more than 400 different creatures that populate their trophy rooms. Hunters receive award trophies for shooting a prescribed list of animals. For example, the "Trophy Animals of Africa" award requires the hunter to kill 79 different African species to win the highest honor.

Animals like elephants and lions are much more valuable alive than dead, to the economies of African nations and to the entire world. An animal can be watched throughout his lifetime, and there's a growing pool of eco-tourism customers waiting for that thrilling experience. On the other hand, the creature targeted by the hunter dies, meaning the revenue gained is merely a one-shot deal. What's more, the pool of people who want to kill elephants, lions, or leopards for fun is comparably tiny, and it's declining. The pictures and the memories for the eco-tourists will last a lifetime, and it's a trip they'll never be ashamed to recount to their grandkids.

Trophy hunting is setting wildlife conservation back, and there are better ways to save these animals than by shooting them.

EVALUATING THE AUTHOR'S ARGUMENTS:

Viewpoint author Teresa Telecky analyzes the issue of trophy hunting in Africa. How would Telecky weigh in on the concept of allowing tribal societies to hunt as is expressed in the previous viewpoint from Survival International?

The Bush Meat Market Shows Hunting's Economic Importance

"Making a real difference... will require manipulating market forces so that more sustainable meats are far cheaper than meat that comes from endangered animals."

Emily Sohn

In the following viewpoint, Emily Sohn analyzes the complicated issue of bush meat hunting in Central Africa. The author maintains that there is a ready market of consumers willing to pay for bush meat, delicacies that may or may not come from endangered species. Sohn details studies that examine the species being killed and that may be pushed to extinction. She also examines possible long-range solutions. Sohn is a freelance journalist writing about science and health and contributes to NPR, among other media outlets.

AS YOU READ, CONSIDER THE FOLLOWING QUESTIONS:
1. What is the definition of bush meat, as stated by Sohn?
2. Which animals are being hunted in particularly high numbers?
3. What health concern is particularly dangerous with bush meat consumption?

"Laws Prohibiting Bush Meat Are Actually a Boon for the Bush Meat Biz," by Emily Sohn, National Public Radio Inc. (NPR), August 14, 2015. Reprinted by permission.

Bush meat may be consumed as subsistence and as luxury food. Aside from endangering species and introducing health risks, the bush meat market offers economic opportunity.

W hat's for dinner?

Porcupines, giant squirrels, dwarf crocodiles and a variety of primates, including golden-bellied crowned monkeys and Bioko black colobus monkeys.

Those are some of the bush meat offerings at the outdoor covered market in Malabo on Bioko Island, part of Equatorial Guinea in Central Africa. And shoppers are willing to pay more for these prized delicacies than they'd fork over for chicken or fish.

Scientists are curious about the impact of the market for wild game, known as bush meat. Are endangered animals being hunted and killed? Is there a growing demand for primates, who could carry diseases that threaten humans?

A new study of the Malabo market offers mostly bad news.

A booming economy has caused an increase in bush meat hunting over a 13-year period, with a particularly sharp rise in the numbers of imperiled monkeys showing up for sale at the market.

Even worse, the study found, efforts to curb killings of those species have repeatedly backfired—producing a temporary lull followed by an even more intense boom once hunters realized they wouldn't face any real consequences.

Those findings highlight some of the challenges in altering a culturally ingrained practice with a complicated array of conservation, economic and health implications.

"We were able to show that it doesn't matter what your intentions are," says Drew Cronin, a primatologist and conservation biologist at Drexel University in Philadelphia. "If you pass a wildlife law and you don't do anything about it, you can actually be doing harm."

Steep and lush, Bioko Island is an idyllic place with a landscape defined by three volcanic peaks. Its tropical rain forests teem with wildlife, including species that live nowhere else. Many of those animals show up dead on a daily basis at the market in Malabo, in the northern part of the island.

Six days a week since the late 1990s, data collectors from the Bioko Biodiversity Protection Program have visited the market to count every animal there. Their records include species names, approximate ages, whether animals were shot or trapped, and if they came from the island or the mainland.

From 1997 to 2010, the team counted a total of 197,000 animals belonging to 28 species, Cronin and colleagues report in PLOS ONE. Sales increased over time as Equatorial Guinea saw an oil boom that fueled economic growth. The average number of primate carcasses counted per day, for example, jumped from four to seventeen over the course of the study period.

A substantial proportion of the animals that are hunted on Bioko end up at the Malabo market, making it a useful indicator of what's happening in the surrounding environment, says John Fa, a conservation scientist and animal ecologist at Manchester Metropolitan University in the United Kingdom, who studied the market on Bioko before the BBPP team took over. Alongside his work, the new study suggests that hunters are decimating certain species. A new road in the southern part of the island is adding concerns, easing access for hunters to even more areas of forest.

"Drew's studies give us more elements to sound the alarm that Bioko Island's animals and in particular its primates need to be protected as soon as possible," Fa says. "Otherwise, they are going to disappear."

Better law enforcement would be one important step to prevent what Cronin calls a "mardi gras mentality." After every major conservation measure has been enacted, the study shows, hunters note an absence of repercussions. They then renew their efforts with extra intensity, perhaps to get whatever meat they can before a new round of legislative or enforcement efforts arrive. After a 2007 ban on primate hunting, for example, numbers of primate carcasses counted at the market per day dropped briefly to almost zero before jumping to thirty-seven per day for several months.

Also essential will be finding viable alternatives for hunters who are resistant to giving up a lucrative trade. A bush meat hunter can make as much as $3,000 a year, Fa says. That's a significant sum in Bioko. Bush meat is more expensive than other meats, he adds, making it a status symbol. The majority of buyers are wealthier people, who prefer the taste to cheaper cuts of pork, beef, chicken or fish. "People are willing to pay enormous amounts of money for bush meat," Fa says, "especially monkeys."

In 2007, a plate of rice, vegetables and half a chicken sold for about $4 US at the market. The researchers believe that at that time, a monkey carcass would have cost ten times as much, and that monkey prices have increased dramatically since then.

Health concerns add another complicated layer to the story. Butchering primates ups the risk for the transmission of diseases like HIV from animals to people. There's another, more chronic health risk involved, too, Fa says. Hunters appear to be using their boost in disposable income to buy soda, beer, cigarettes, junk food and other products that aren't good for them.

Cronin and his team are working toward solutions on Bioko by stationing more wildlife guards in the island's national park in the north, among other steps. The new study also notes that certain remote areas of the island have remained untouched, so he's hopeful.

Still, efforts elsewhere to introduce beekeeping, wildlife farming or other new ways of life to hunters have been miserable failures, Fa says. Making a real difference, he suspects, will require manipulating market forces so that more sustainable meats are far cheaper than meat that comes from endangered animals. At the same time, there will need to be a strong educational program to reduce the demand for wild meat.

"This study," Fa says, "must be seen as a window into how things can go from bad to worse because of economic situations."

EVALUATING THE AUTHOR'S ARGUMENTS:

Viewpoint author Emily Sohn reports on efforts to replace the economic system of hunting and selling bush meat. What strategies have already been tried according to the viewpoint, and what were the results? Brainstorm two other ideas that could possibly provide results.

Hunting Is Its Own Endangered Species

Noble Research Institute

"Currently, the public is mostly undecided on whether hunting is moral, a wholesome activity or still involves the sportsmanlike pursuit of animals."

In the following viewpoint, Noble Research Institute proposes that the future of hunting will be decided by non-hunters. The author analyses several reasons why hunting may eventually become obsolete and provides suggestions for hunters to turn this tide to a favorable position for their sport. The authors suggest that hunters, predominantly men, take others, including women and young people out into the field to get them interested in hunting. Noble Research Institute is an organization of over 400 scientists, researchers, and others conducting agricultural research, and solving problems for farmers and ranchers.

AS YOU READ, CONSIDER THE FOLLOWING QUESTIONS:

1. In matters of hunting, what effects occur when most people do not live in rural settings?
2. What three factors may decide the fate of hunting?
3. As stated in the viewpoint, what are today's youth doing instead of hunting?

"The Future of Hunting Is in Danger," Noble Research Institute, LLC, November 1, 2009. Reprinted by permission.

Introducing younger generations to the joys and responsibilities of the sport of hunting could help keep the tradition alive.

The year is 2015 and after years of debate among conservation organizations, pro-hunting organizations, animal rights activists and antihunting groups, all forms of hunting in the United States have been banned by the federal government. Is this a real possibility? In my opinion, the answer is yes. Regardless of what some people think, hunting is an opportunity that can be taken away and those who will ultimately decide its fate are the non-hunting public. Currently, the public is mostly undecided on whether hunting is moral, a wholesome activity or still involves the sportsmanlike pursuit of animals.

There are about 12.5 million hunters over the age of 16 in the US. It is vital for hunters, both individually and as a group, to demonstrate that hunting is a moral and wholesome activity. This is increasingly difficult because more and more people are further removed from rural lifestyles. Fewer immedi-

ate family members are involved in hunting or agriculture where the birth, care and death of animals are parts of daily life. Lessons from the farm are largely lost on today's generation, including hunters.

The fate of hunting will be influenced by at least three factors. First, hunters need to police their own ranks and not ignore questionable acts of other hunters. Secondly, hunters need to communicate more effectively with non-hunting groups. Lastly, to be sustainable, the sport needs new hunters.

Policing our ranks should not emphasize internal debates over archery, muzzle loader or rifle seasons or equipment choice. These things are minor compared to hunters holding one another accountable to ethical and high moral conduct. We can't ignore activities such as poaching and trespassing. Additionally, appropriate conduct extends to the concept of "fair chase" or avoiding the use of technology, gadgets or practices that gives unfair advantage to hunters over the animals being pursued.

Drs. Michael Nelson and Kelly Millenbah published an article in the fall 2009 issue of *Wildlife Professional* proposing that there may be more common ground between ethical hunters and non-hunters than either group thinks. They point out that, in the debate over the ethics of hunting, dialogue has been replaced by dogmatism, honesty by hostility and progress by platitudes. However, they suggest that a common ground exists: respect for animals. They go on to say that most anti-hunters simply want hunters to demonstrate respect for the animals they hunt and to acknowledge that animals have moral standing. They propose that "wildlife professionals and hunters could recognize the direct moral standing of animals and work to unite this recognition with the possibility of hunting and eating animals."

With the increasing commercialization of hunting and wildlife, the potential grows for this industry to substitute "entertainment" and a "positive experience" for traditional values and ethical concepts, such as fair chase. Some aspects of commercialization, e.g., canned hunts and gadgetry, will appeal to those who are shortsighted and are not vested in the outcome of hunting. Time in the field is at a premium and, with companies offering gadgets and canned hunts that promise increased odds of harvesting an animal... well, money talks.

Statistics show that hunter numbers are declining annually. Probable factors are too numerous to look into here. Traditionally, hunting has been a male-dominated activity, but this is changing. More and more women are taking up and enjoying hunting. In regards to youth, hunting seems to be overshadowed by video games, television, computers and organized activities such as sports and music. An increasing number of youth are not being taught that death is a part of life and that game animals are a renewable resource. It is important that youth and women become involved and participate in hunting and that hunting mentors teach them what fair chase and ethical conduct is all about.

Take a child hunting. Invite your spouse, sister, aunt or a neighbor to spend some time in the field to share your knowledge regarding the importance of respecting animals, hunting ethically, observing sportsmanship and maintaining wildlife habitat. Who is a better mentor than an ethical, knowledgeable and conservation minded sportsman? The future of hunting depends on you.

EVALUATING THE AUTHOR'S ARGUMENTS:

In this viewpoint, the author at Noble Research Institute analyzes the issues surrounding the potential ban of hunting. Do you hunt, or know someone who does hunt? Outline a case for or against a ban on hunting using the viewpoints you've read in this resource.

Viewpoint 7

Tourism and Conservation Can Work Together

"Observations of several deer species have found that they are more abundant in the conservation area than outside it."

United Nations Environment Programme

In the following excerpted viewpoint, the United Nations Environment Programme (UNEP) makes a case for a type of tourism called wildlife watching. Trips planned around wildlife watching, in which travelers experience wildlife in their natural habitat, have been proven to impact wildlife species in a positive way. This is because the trips and tours contribute economically to the cause, and also they bring attention to the species. The United Nations Environment Programme is a branch of the United Nations that coordinates its environmental activities.

AS YOU READ, CONSIDER THE FOLLOWING QUESTIONS:
1. What is wildlife watching tourism, according to the viewpoint?
2. How does wildlife watching differ from ecotourism?
3. How were funds raised for whale conservation in the Seychelles?

"Wildlife Watching and Tourism," United Nations Environment Programme (UNEP). ©UNEP/CMS Wildlife Watching and Tourism. Reprinted by permission.

Commercial whaling is still permitted in Iceland and Norway, despite the fact that many whale species are endangered. Eco-tourism could be a solution to avoiding extinction.

W hat is wildlife watching and how does it relate to tourism? Wildlife is a general term that technically covers both flora and fauna, although in popular use, wildlife is mostly used to refer to animals in the wild. Perhaps a classic image of wildlife for many people is a large mammal or a flock of wild birds, but the term is widely used to cover all types of animals, including all kinds of insects, and marine life.

Wildlife watching is simply an activity that involves the watching of wildlife. It is normally used to refer to the watching of animals, and this distinguishes wildlife watching from other forms of wildlife-based activities, such as hunting and fishing. Watching wild-life and animals is essentially an observational activity, although in some cases it can involve interactions with the animals being watched, such as touching or feeding them.

Wildlife watching tourism is then tourism that is organised and undertaken in order to watch wildlife. This type of tourism has grown dramatically in recent years, and a quick search on the internet provides many examples of tourism companies that either market specific wildlife watching tours, or promote their products by highlighting wildlife watching as an optional activity that their clients can enjoy.

The tourism industry tends to use the term "wildlife tourism" rather than wildlife watching tourism. In many cases, the two terms are identical, but wildlife tourism is sometimes also used to refer to hunting or fishing tourism, and in a few cases to the viewing of captive wildlife in zoos or confined parks where the animals no longer live a wild existence.[1]   [...]

Wildlife watching particularly overlaps with ecotourism, which is a form of tourism based on the principles[2] of making an active contribution to the conservation of natural and cultural heritage; involving local and indigenous communities in its planning development and operation, and contributing to their well-being; and interpreting natural and cultural heritage to visitors. Ecotourism is often based on relatively low levels of tourism in an area, and is therefore particularly suited to organised tours for small groups, and also for independent travellers.

[...]

Examples from around the world show how tourism has been used successfully to help fund conservation activities, and through this, to protect wildlife and habitats that might otherwise have been destroyed or subjected to alternative uses with far greater environmental impacts. For example, conservationists set up crocodile watching safaris on the Black River in Jamaica to protect the crocodile population which was threatened by poaching. Projeto Tamar has successfully promoted the conservation of turtles along the Brazilian coastline, and has helped to improve turtle numbers by protecting hatcheries—introducing more than 600,000 turtle hatchlings to the sea in 2003 alone. Projeto Tamar has achieved this by working with local communities and fishermen to establish alternative employment and income streams based on turtle protection.

In the Annapurna Conservation Area in Nepal, where tourism is an important activity, observations of several deer species have found that they are more abundant in the conservation area than outside it.[3] A census of mountain gorillas in the Democratic Republic of Congo (DRC), Rwanda and Uganda, has found that the population is increasing, and that the greatest increase is evident in gorilla groups that are habituated for tourism and regularly visited. In Península Valdés, Argentina, the whale population is increasing and the high number of mother-calf pairs in nursery grounds there suggest that they are unaffected by current whale watching activities.

In the Galapagos Islands and Bunaken National Marine Park, wildlife watching tourism provides all or most of the annual budget for park management, including the costs of managing tourism. In the Seychelles, whale shark watching is used to raise the funds needed for monitoring and research for whale shark conservation.

In Mexico, conservation of the main overwintering sites for Monarch butterflies, which together cover only a few hundred hectares, has been integrated with a much larger project—the Monarch Butterfly Model Forest—focused on improving livelihoods and income-generation opportunities for people and communities throughout an area of 300 km x 250 km. The project has promoted community development and protection of forests and environmental resources throughout this region, as well as restoring critical Monarch Butterfly overwintering habitat, and providing training in ecotourism for local people.

These examples and others like them, show how tourism, conservation and community development can work together. [...]

Notes

1. *Wildlife Tourism: Impacts, Management and Planning*, (2004) Edited by Karen Higginbottom, published by Common Ground Publishing Pty Ltd, Australia; Wildlife Tourism, (2005), David Newsome, Ross Dowling and Susan Moore, Aspects of Tourism no. 24, published by Channel View Publications.
2. Quebec Declaration on Ecotourism, 2002.
3. B.B. Siddhartha, P.A. Furley, and A.C. Newton (2005) "Effectiveness of community involvement in delivering conservation benefits to the Annapurna Conservation Area, Nepal," Environmental Conservation 32 (3): 239–247.

EVALUATING THE AUTHOR'S ARGUMENTS:

The United Nations Environment Programme makes a compelling case for the benefits of wildlife tourism in promoting conservation efforts around the world.

Facts About Hunting

Editor's note: These facts can be used in reports to add credibility when making important points or claims.

Facts that Support Hunting

In the mid 1800's American hunters and anglers urged for conservation—the North American Wildlife Conservation Model was developed and is the only one in the world.

- Two Basic Principles: America's fish and wildlife belongs to all and their populations will be sustained forever.
- Seven guidelines to achieve this management:
    1. Wildlife is Held in the Public Trust
    2. Prohibition on Commerce of Dead Wildlife
    3. Democratic Rule of Law
    4. Hunting Opportunity for All
    5. Non-Frivolous Use
    6. International Resources
    7. Scientific Management
- The Pittman-Robertson Wildlife Restoration Act and the Dingell-Johnson Act (two laws that mandate collection of money from hunters). Approximately 1 billion per year is collected from arms and ammunition used for hunting and equipment used for fishing and this money is used to support wildlife conservation. In 2018, 1.1 billion from these taxes will be distributed to state wildlife agencies for conservation efforts.
- In 2016, more than 35.8 million Americans went fishing, 11.5 million hunted and 86 million watched wildlife.
- In 2016, 14% of Americans (older than 16) fished, 5% hunted and 35% watched wildlife.
- In 2016, more than 101 million American, around 40% of the US population participated in some fishing, hunting, birdwatching or outdoor photography.

- In 2013, 48% of Americans had guns for protection, and 32% for hunting.
- In 2013, 79% of Americans favored hunting according to a national poll.
- Hunters must purchase a license from the state in which they hunt.
- In 1903, President Theodore Roosevelt created the first wildlife refuge in the US.
- In 1949, Conservationist Aldo Leopold publishes his landmark book on conservation and wildlife, *A Sand County Almanac.*

Anti-hunting Facts

- PETA is the largest animal rights organization in the world, is anti-hunting, and has a worldwide following and support of over 6.5 million members.
- In 1962, Rachel Carson publishes *Silent Spring,* her landmark book warning about a possible coming wildlife calamity—the disappearance of all things wild and natural.
- In 1973, the Endangered Species Act was enacted. It provided for the conservation of ecosystems upon which threatened and endangered species of fish, wildlife, and plants depend.
- In 2013, 12% of Americans were against hunting according to a national poll.
- Over 90% of National Wildlife Refuge lands were set aside for the public (not paid for by hunting revenue).
- Less than 3% of National Wildlife Refuge lands were paid for by hunting revenue such as funds from the National Migratory Bird Conservation fund.
- Many hunters oppose a ban on lead ammunition (lead is poisonous to animals and people).
- Hunters tend to seek out trophy animals (biggest tusks, antlers, horns), while in nature, the old, sick, and weak animals die (trophy animals would be better for the health of the wild population).

Organizations to Contact

The editors have compiled the following list of organizations concerned with the issues debated in this book. The descriptions are derived from materials provided by the organizations. All have publications or information available for interested readers. The list was compiled on the date of publication of the present volume; the information provided here may change. Be aware that many organizations take several weeks or longer to respond to inquiries, so allow as much time as possible for the receipt of requested materials.

Association of Fish & Wildlife Agencies (AFWA)
1100 First Street NE, Suite 825, Washington, DC 20002
(202) 838-3474
email: info@fishwildlife.org
website: www.fishwildlife.org
AFWA is an association of America's fish and wildlife agencies. They aim to provide science-based conservation and management of America's fish and wildlife, and the necessary habitat to conserve these natural resources for all citizens.

Congressional Sportsmen's Foundation (CSF)
110 North Caroline Avenue, SE, Washington, DC 20003
(202) 543-6850
email: csf@congressionalsportsmen.org
website: http://congressionalsportsmen.org/
Congressional Sportsmen's Foundation has been active since 1989. CSF's focus is to work with Congress, governors, and state legislatures to advance and protect the issues of hunting, fishing, recreational shooting, and trapping.

Ducks Unlimited, INC. (DU)
One Waterfowl Way, Memphis, TN 38120
1-800-45DUCKS
email: contact through the website

website: www.ducks.org

Ducks Unlimited is an organization focused on wetland and water-fowl (ducks, geese, swans) conservation. The mission of DU is to manage, restore, and conserve habitat for America's waterfowl, which increases waterfowl populations to benefit wildlife and people, including waterfowl hunters.

National Audubon Society

225 Varick St, 7th Fl.

New York, NY 10014

(212) 979-3196

email: audubon@emailcustomerservice.com

website: www.audobon.org

Using science, advocacy, education, and grassroots conservation, the National Audobon Society protects wildlife in the Americas. The nonprofit's experts guide lawmakers and agencies in shaping conservation plans and actions. The society owns and operates nature centers in urban centers such as New York City and Los Angeles.

National Rifle Association (NRA)

11250 Waple Mills Road, Fairfax, VA 22030

1-800-672-3888

email: contact through the website

website: explore.nra.org

The NRA is a national organization dedicated to providing US law abiding citizens the ability to acquire and keep firearms. The agency focuses on helping hunters in many ways, and actively promotes hunting, and acts against anti-hunting interests. The NRA produces a magazine, the *American Rifleman,* which is the largest firearm magazine in the world.

People for The Ethical Treatment of Animals (PETA)

501 Front Street, Norfolk, VA 23510

757-622-PETA

email: contact through the website

website: www.peta.org/

PETA is a worldwide organization dedicated to the protection of animals. It has a membership of supporters, over 6.5 million strong. PETA focuses their attention on four areas they feel are most important for the protection of animals: animals in the food industry, in entertainment, in clothing, and in laboratories. PETA's website lists many opportunities for getting involved.

Sierra Club

National Headquarters, 2101 Webster St. Suite 1300, Oakland, CA, 94612
(415) 977-5500
email: information@sierraclub.org
website: www.sierraclub.org
The Sierra Club is the nation's largest environmental organization founded by the famous conservationist John Muir in 1892. The agency has helped protect millions of acres of wilderness, and get the Clean Air, Clean Water, and Endangered Species Acts passed. In hunting related areas the Sierra Club projects a strong stance against using hounds for hunting bears and bobcats and is also against all trapping. The *Sierra Club Insider* is a twice-monthly e-newsletter keeps interested people updated on the latest environmental news.

The Humane Society of the United States (HSUS)

1255 23rd Street, NW, Suite 450, Washington, DC 20037
(202) 452-1100
email: donorcare@humanesociety.org
website: www.humanesociety.org
The Humane Society of the United States, advertises itself as the most effective animal protection organization in the world. The agency provides hands-on care and services to more than 100,000 animals per year and concentrates on combatting a variety of animal cruelty throughout the world including captive hunts, wildlife trade, and many other animal threats. HSUS furthers its mission by publishing two informational magazines: *All Animals* for members, and *Animal Sheltering* for professionals.

United States Fish & Wildlife Service (USFWS)

1849 C Street, NW, Washington, DC 20240

1-800-344-WILD
email: contact through the website
website: www.fws.gov/
The US Fish & Wildlife Service works with many other agencies to protect, enhance, and conserve the wildlife, fish, plants and habitats of natural areas for the benefit of the American people. This agency manages the National Wildlife Refuge System, migratory birds, animals and fish including endangered species, and enforces the laws protecting those identities.

Wildlife Defense League (WDL)
P.O. Box 30038, North Vancouver, British Columbia V7H 2Y8
email: wildlifedefenseleague@gmail.com
website: www.wildlifedefenceleague.org/
The mission of the Wildlife Defense League is to stop the exploitation of wildlife in British Columbia. Through education, community outreach, and active campaigns the WDL seeks to limit and/or end trophy hunting of species such as grizzly bears.

For Further Reading

Books

Blood, Hal. *Hunting Big Woods Bucks: Secrets of Tracking and Stalking Whitetails.* New York, NY: Skyhorse Publishing Company Inc., 2012.

Details all the techniques and tips for tracking White-tailed deer to have a successful hunting experience.

Goodall, Jane. *Hope for Animals and Their World: How Endangered Species are Being Rescued from the Brink.* New York, NY: Grand Central Publishing, 2009.

Interweaving her own personal stories with those of other research scientists, renowned scientist Jane Goodall paints a picture of hope about the survival of animals. Also details how environmentalists are saving important animal habitats.

Hanson, John Marvin. *Hunting camp 52: Tales from a North Woods Deer Camp.* Madison, WI: Wisconsin Society Historical Press, 2016.

Provides an interesting look into different aspects of deer hunting in northern Wisconsin.

Lock, Deborah. *Secrets of the Cave.* New York, NY: DK Publishing, 2015.

Experience the grandeur and excitement of the prehistoric cave painters of Lascaux, France. Sense the danger and drama facing prehistoric hunters by witnessing the animals they revered and hunted for sustenance.

Lunde, Darrin P. *The Naturalist: Theodore Roosevelt, a Lifetime of Exploration, and the Triumph of American Natural History.* New York, NY: Crown Publishers, 2016.

Shares the triumph of natural history and conservation that came about as a result of Theodore Roosevelt. Also details the biographical journey of Roosevelt from a boyhood of hunting and naturalist activities to adulthood.

O'Connor, M.R. *Resurrection Science: Conservation, De-extinction and the Precarious Future of Wild Things.* New York, NY: St. Martin's Press, 2015.

Analyzes current biological controversy surrounding the possibility of bringing back previously extinct animals.

Orenstein, Ronald I. *Ivory, Horn and Blood: Behind the Elephant and Rhinoceros Poaching Crisis.* ON, CA: Firefly Books, 2013.

Presents historical background and current information about the poaching of elephants and rhinoceros. Gives insight into the laws attempting to curb poaching, why people poach, what encourages poaching, and what can be done.

Tucker, Linda. *Saving the White Lions: One Woman's Battle for Africa's Most Sacred Animal.* Berkeley, CA: North Atlantic Books, 2013.

Conservationist Linda Tucker writes about her struggle to save and protect the white lions in Africa from trophy hunters.

Underwood, Lamar. *The Greatest Hunting Stories Ever Told.* Guilford, CT: Lyons Press, 2000.

Provides a compilation of hunting stories from famous hunters such as Ernest Hemingway and Theodore Roosevelt. It depicts a variety of animals hunted in various habitats.

Periodicals and Internet Sources

Actman, Jani, & Bale, Rachael, "How Wildlife May Fare Under Trump," *National Geographic*, November, 2016. https://news.nationalgeographic.com/2016/11/wildlife-watch-trump-wildlife-trafficking-animal-conservation/?_ga=2.34249064.815521866.1524326907-867846833.1524078221.

Ames, Marissa, "Rat-Hunting Dogs: A Historically Organic Option," Countryside Daily, April, 2018. https://countrysidenetwork.com/daily/homesteading/pests-predators/rat-hunting-dogs-a-historically-organic-option/.

Bale, Rachael, "On the Trail of Jaguar Poachers," *National Geographic*, December, 2017. https://www.nationalgeographic.com/magazine/2017/12/on-the-trail-of-jaguar-poachers/.

Cosgrove, Ben, "Life at Lascaux: First Color Photos From Another

World," *Time*, May, 2014. http://time.com/3879943/lascaux-early-color-photos-of-the-famous-cave-paintings-france-1947/.

Cruise, Adam, "Is Trophy Hunting Helping Save African Elephants?" *National Geographic*, November, 2015. https://news.nationalgeographic.com/2015/11/151715-conservation-trophy-hunting-elephants-tusks-poaching-zimbabwe-namibia/.

Daley, Jason, "Where the Ice Age Caribou Ranged," *Archaeology*, December, 2017. https://www.archaeology.org/issues/281-1801/features/6162-where-the-ice-age-caribou-ranged.

Elgin, Beckie, "Hounding the Hunters," *Earth Island Journal*, Winter, 2016. http://www.earthisland.org/journal/index.php/eij/article/hounding_the_hunters/.

Enders, Caty, "Hunting Class is Now in Session," *Outdoor Life*, January, 2018. https://www.outdoorlife.com/hunting-class-is-now-in-session.

Flocken, Jeffrey, "Trophy Hunting: Killing Animals to Save Them is Not Conservation," CNN, January, 2018. https://www.cnn.com/2015/05/19/opinions/trophy-hunting-not-conservation-flocken/index.html.

Franz, Julia, "Why Did Passenger Pigeons Go Extinct," PRI, December, 2017. https://www.pri.org/stories/2017-12-03/why-did-passenger-pigeons-go-extinct.

Garth, Gary, "Wild Turkeys: A Conservation (and Hunting) Success Story," *USA Today*, March, 2017. https://www.usatoday.com/story/travel/destinations/2017/03/09/wild-turkey-hunting/98902394/.

Lalire, Gregory, "Buffalo Business," History Net, January, 2018. http://www.historynet.com/letter-wild-west-april-2018.htm.

Lanchester, John, "The Case Against Civilization," *The New Yorker*, September, 2017. https://www.newyorker.com/magazine/2017/09/18/the-case-against-civilization.

Larson, Christina, "The End of Hunting," *Washington Monthly*, January/February, 2006. http://www.christina-larson.com/the-end-of-hunting/.

Paterniti, Michael, "Should We Kill Animals to Save Them?" *National Geographic*, October, 2017. https://www.nationalgeographic.com/magazine/2017/10/trophy-hunting-killing-saving-animals/.

Yeoman, Barry, "Why the Passenger Pigeon Went Extinct," *Audubon*, May/June, 2014. http://www.audubon.org/magazine/may-june-2014/why-passenger-pigeon-went-extinct.

Zorich, Zach, "New Dates for the Oldest Cave Paintings," *Archaeology*, June, 2016. https://www.archaeology.org/issues/221-1607/trenches/4551-trenches-france-chauvet-dating.

Websites
National Geographic
www.natgeokids.com/nz/discover/science/nature/conservation-tips/#!/register
National Geographic conservation tips for kids site details 5 ways for kids to be conservation minded. Avoiding products with palm oil for instance improves chances for elephants, orangutans, and gorillas.

National Geographic
kids.nationalgeographic.com/explore/nature/mission-animal-rescue/
Mission Animal Rescue provides kids an access for learning about animals and resources and activities to take action to save threatened and endangered animals.

PETA KIDS
www.petakids.com/
PETA KIDS encourages kids to learn all about animals and how to protect them. Site includes videos, games, and articles about wild animals and companion animals.

US Fish and Wildlife Service Conservation Kids
www.fws.gov/international/education-zone/conservation-kids.html
Conservation Kids site hosted by the US Fish & Wildlife service is a place to find out about many topics concerned with hunting and conservation in the US and around the world.

Index

A

agriculture, 8, 11, 12, 18, 31, 59, 66, 101
All About Wildlife, 29–32
ancestors, 13, 14, 15, 30, 31, 53
Anderson, Terry, 46–51
animal welfare, 51
Audubon, John James, 8, 76

B

bush meat hunting, 94–98

C

canned hunts, 9, 40, 43, 102
Capps, Ashley, 68–71
carnivores, 14, 56, 82
causations, 84
commercialization, 102
confirmation bias, 38
cruelty, 43
cultural traditions, 23, 37

D

Dallas Safari Club, 47, 90–91, 92
Darwin, Charles, 8
deforestation, 59, 62
driven hunt, 26
Duclos, Joshua, 33–38

E

Endangered Species Act, 47, 91, 108

evolution, 12, 68, 71
extinction, 9, 41, 52, 56, 58, 59, 60, 63, 77, 79, 94

F

family hunting tips, 21
farming, 11, 12, 15, 69, 71, 98
fishing, 7, 8, 15, 53, 55, 104, 107
food production, 7, 11, 12

H

Hosmer, Joe, 64–67
human population, 7, 25, 50, 60
hunter-gatherers, 8, 11
hunting
    be allowed, 85–88
    benefits of, 64–67
    contradiction, 13
    facts about, 107–108
    for survival, 7, 8, 13, 40
    future of, 99–102
    good for conservation, 48
    impact of outlawing, 87–88
    is natural, 7, 33, 37
    not fair chase, 55
    not sport, 55
    pain and suffering, 41–42, 52, 53, 54
    rationales for, 35, 52
    regulated, 67
    as tradition, 16–22, 24–28
    what bothers people, 35–37

I

illegal hunting, 46, 50, 58, 59
In Defense of Animals, 52–57
  what you can do, 57
International Council for Game
  and Wildlife Conservation
  (CIC), 28
invasive species, 80, 82

L

Lester, Liza, 80–84
Loomis, Vern, 11–15

M

Migratory Bird Treaty Act, 79
morality, 33, 34, 37

N

National Audubon Society, 44,
  45, 57, 73
National Park System, 9
natural predators, 42–43,
  52, 55, 56
Noble Research
  Institute, 99–102

P

passenger pigeon, 74–79
People for the Ethical Treatment
  of Animals (PETA), 7,
  40–45, 57, 108
  what you can do, 44
Pittman-Robertson Act,
  65–66, 107
poaching, 7, 42, 46, 49, 58, 59,
  60–61, 85, 87, 101, 105
  facts about, 61–63

population control, 55, 56, 70
prehistoric cave art, 9,
  29, 31–32
Project Passenger Pigeon, 74–76

R

Raised Hunting, 16–22
reverse evolution, 68, 71
Roosevelt, Theodore, 8–9, 108

S

Sierra Club, 44
Sohn, Emily, 94–98
sport hunting, 35, 36, 40,
  44, 45, 55
subsistence hunting, 15, 35, 62
Supeková, Soňa, 23–28
survival, 7–8, 11, 12, 13, 15, 31,
  35, 36, 40, 41, 42, 53, 54,
  66, 77, 78, 91, 92
Survival International, 85–88
sustainable management, 25, 65

T

Telecky, Teresa M., 89–93
therapeutic hunting, 35, 36
totem animals, 86
tribal societies, 85–88
  myths, 87
trophy hunting, 9, 89–93

U

United Nations Environment
  Programme, 103–106
urbanization, 25
US Fish and Wildlife Service, 7,
  47, 63, 65, 82, 90, 101

W

wildlife conservation, 25,
    46–51, 55–56, 57, 64,
    91, 93, 107
wildlife farming, 98
wildlife tourism, 104, 105
wildlife trade, 59, 60, 61, 63
wildlife watching, 103–106
women in hunting, 27–28, 66,
    67, 99, 102
World Animal
    Foundation, 58–63
World Wildlife Fund (WWF),
    7, 44, 57, 66

Y

Yeoman, Barry, 73–79

Picture Credits